BOOKS BY ROBERT PENN WARREN

John Brown: The Making of a Martyr

Thirty-six Poems

Night Rider

Eleven Poems on the Same Theme

At Heaven's Gate

Selected Poems, 1923–1943

All the King's Men

Blackberry Winter

The Circus in the Attic

World Enough and Time

Brother to Dragons

Band of Angels

Segregation: The Inner Conflict in the South

Promises: Poems 1954–1956

Selected Essays

The Cave

All the King's Men (play)

You, Emperors, and Others: Poems 1957–1960

The Legacy of the Civil War

Wilderness

Flood

Who Speaks for the Negro?

Selected Poems: New and Old 1923–1966

Incarnations: Poems 1966–1968

Audubon: A Vision

Homage to Theodore Dreiser

HOMAGE TO THEODORE DREISER

HOMAGE TO
Theodore
Dreiser

August 27, 1871 — December 28, 1945
ON THE CENTENNIAL OF HIS BIRTH

✠✠

ROBERT
PENN
WARREN

RANDOM HOUSE
New York

ISBN: 0-394-41027-0
Library of Congress Catalog Card Number: 73-156965

Printed and bound in the United States of America
by Haddon Craftsmen, Scranton, Pennsylvania
First Edition

To previous writers on Dreiser I owe many obvious debts, and gratefully acknowledge them. More immediately I am deeply obligated to R. W. B. Lewis, C. Vann Woodward, Dr. Albert Rothenberg, Mrs. Neda Westlake, of the Charles Patterson Van Pelt Library of the University of Pennsylvania, Bernard Karpel, Librarian of the Museum of Modern Art, of New York City, and Richard W. Dowell, editor of the *Dreiser Newsletter*, of Indiana University, at Terre Haute. And I must acknowledge, with gratitude, the permission of the University of Pennsylvania to reprint here unpublished material from the Theodore Dreiser Collection.

R. P. W.

Fairfield, March 10, 1971

TO

VANN AND GLENN WOODWARD

Whatever flames upon the night
Man's own resinous heart has fed.

W. B. YEATS

—then on the shore
Of the wide world I stand alone, and think,
Till love and fame to nothingness do sink.

JOHN KEATS

HOMAGE TO THEODORE DREISER

From "On the Banks of the Wabash, Far Away";
words by Theodore Dreiser and Paul Dresser, music by Paul Dresser.

PORTRAIT

I. PSYCHOLOGICAL PROFILE

Who is the ugly one slump-slopping down the street?
Who is the chinless wonder with the potato-nose?
Can't you hear the soft plop *of the pancake-shaped feet?*

He floats, like Anchises' son, in the cloud of his fine new clothes,
Safe, safe at last, from the street's sneer, toward
                              a queen who will fulfill
The fate devised him by Venus—but where, oh when! That
                              is what he never knows.

Born with one hand in his pants and one in the till,
He knows that the filth of self, to be loved, must be clad in glory,
So once stole twenty-five dollars to buy a new coat, and
                              that is why still

The left eye keeps squinting backward—yes, history
Is gumshoeing closer behind, with the constable-hand
                              that clutches.
Watch his mouth, how it moves without sound, he is
                              telling himself his own old story.

From lies, masturbation, vainglory, and shame,
He moves in his dream of ladies swan-necked, with
                              asses ample and sweet,
But knows that no kiss heals his soul, it is always the same.

Full of screaming his soul is, and a stench like live
                              flesh that scorches.
It's a screaming, and stench, like a horse-barn afire,
And the great beasts rear and utter, their manes flare
                              up like torches.

But he hears a brass band in the distance, and
                              the midnight cricket,
Though thinly, asseverates his name. He seeks amid
                              the day's traffic a sign—

‡ 3 ‡

Some horseshoe or hunchback or pin—that now, at last,
                                        at the end of this street

He will enter upon his reality: but enters only in-
To your gut, or your head, or your heart, to enhouse
                                        there and stay,
And in that hot darkness lie lolling and swell—like a tumor,
                                        perhaps benign.

May I present Mr. Dreiser? He will write a great novel, someday.

‡ 4 ‡

II. VITAL STATISTICS

Past Terre Haute, the diesels pound,
Eastward, westward, and under the highway slab the ground,
Like jello, shakes. Deep
In the infatuate and foetal dark, beneath
The unspecifiable weight of the great
Mid-America loam-sheet, the impacted
Particular particles of loam, blind,
Minutely grind.

At that depth and with that weight,
The particles, however minutely, vibrate
At the incessant passage
Of the transcontinental truck freight,
And concerning that emperor whose gut was god, Tacitus
Wrote "ex urbe atque Italia inritamenta gulae gestabantur . . . ,"
And from both
Adriatic and Tyrrhenian seas, sea-crayfish and bivalve and,
Glare-eyed, the mullet, redder than flame,
Surrendered themselves in delight
To soothe the soft gullet wheredown all honor and empire
Slid slick, and wheels all night
Hummed on the highways to guarantee prompt delivery.

Saliva gathers in the hot darkness of mouth-tissue. The mouth,
Slack, drools at the corners, but ever so little.

Terre Haute lies

On the banks of the Wabash, far away, and tires
On the concrete, scream. In Terre Haute,

Long before the age of the internal combustion engine, but not
Before that of gewgaw, gilt, and grab, when the war
For freedom had just given place to the war for the dollar,
Theodore Dreiser was born. That was on South Ninth Street, but
The exact address is, of course, lost. He was born
Into the vast anonymity of the poor.

        Have you ever
Seen moonlight on the Wabash, far away?

         He was born
On the wrong side of the tracks, and his sisters
Had hot crotches and round heels.
He knew the gnaw of hunger, how the first wind of winter feels,
He was born into the age of conspicuous consumption, and knew
How the heart, in longing, numbly congeals.

Nothing could help nothing, not reading Veblen or even Freud, for
The world is a great ass propped high on pillows, the cunt
Winks.

   Dreiser,
However, could not feel himself worthy. Not,
At least, of love. His nails,
Most horribly, were bitten. At night,
Sometimes, he wept. The bed springs
Creaked with the shift of his body, which,
In the Age of Faith and of Contempt of the World,
Would have been called a sack
Of stercorry: i.e., that matter the body ejects.

Sometimes he wept for the general human condition,
But he was hell on women.

He had never loved any woman, he confessed,
Except his mother, whose broken shoes, he,

‡ 6 ‡

In childhood, had once caressed,
In the discovery of pity.

                    Have you ever
Seen midnight moonlight on the Wabash,
While the diesel rigs boom by?
Have you ever thought how the moonlit continent
Would look from the tearless and unblinking distance of
                                        God's wide eye?

‡ 7 ‡

III. MORAL ASSESSMENT

No psychiatrist need be called
To anatomize his pain.
He suffers but the kind all men
Suffer in their human kind.
No—suffers, too,
His nobility of mind.

He denies it, he sneers at it,
In his icy nightmare of
The superlative of self;
And tries, but cannot theorize past
The knowledge that
Others suffer, too, at last.

He is no philosopher.
His only gift is to enact
All that his deepest self abhors,
And learn, in his self-contempting distress,
The secret worth
Of all our human worthlessness.

The career of Theodore Dreiser raises in a peculiarly poignant form the question of the relation of life and art. The fiction Dreiser wrote is so much like the life he led that sometimes we are hard put to say exactly what Dreiser—the artist—added to what Dreiser—the man—had observed and experienced. It is tempting to think of him as a kind of uninspired recorder blundering along in a dreary effort to transcribe actuality. And the next temptation is to think that what is good is good by the accident of the actuality that he happened to live into—not by any power that he, as artist, might have achieved.

What is wrong with this way of thinking is, of course, that it does not account for the fact that, in one sense, art is the artist's way of understanding—of creating even—the actuality that he lives. In some artists this process is so complex and indirect, and the result so far from being a document, that the creative aspect is beyond dispute. But with some, as with Dreiser, it is so direct, and the factual correspondences so precise, that we may feel that to try to see his art as a creation of actuality is stupid. And to compound the problem, Dreiser did write voluminously in the form of straight autobiography about himself and his work; and often these autobiographical writings are scarcely distinguishable from his fiction.

Dreiser was, as F. O. Matthiessen, one of his biographers, once remarked in conversation, the first American writer from "across the tracks." That is, he was the first writer not of the old American tradition. Some writers, Whittier for instance, had been born poor, or like Mark Twain and Melville, had had little formal education, but such men felt themselves the inheritors of the civilization they had been born into. Even Whittier, born poor and raised on a rocky farm, was anything but the "peasant poet" he has sometimes been called; the Whittiers, if in a modest way, had been among the founding fathers of New England, and the young Whittier, for all his Quakerism, was burning with ambition to take his rightful place in the great world.

Theodore Dreiser was, however, the immigrant, and though he himself had been born in America, his family was not of that world. He was the outsider, the rejected, the yearner, and that fact conditions the basic emotions and the basic power of his work.

John Paul Dreiser, from Mayen, Germany, a weaver by trade, had come to America well before the Civil War, gone to Ohio, and there married the illiterate, sixteen-year-old daughter of a Moravian farm family, Sarah Schänäb. In those years it seemed that John Paul would achieve the classic success of the industrious immigrant; he operated a woolen mill and had every reason to think that he would prosper. But the mill burned, with no insurance on it or on the wool consigned by local farmers; shortly thereafter he was himself injured, and to complete the disastrous picture, his wife, while he was incapacitated, was stripped of all remaining resources by "Yankee trickery."

Theodore Dreiser was later to feel that man is a pawn in the hands of a blind or malevolent fate, and it may reasonably be guessed that the germ of his philosophy, like that of Herman Melville, lay in the early disaster of the father. And if a secret drama of Melville's work is the search for the father who died after failure, a secret drama of Dreiser's is the rejection of a father who, after failure, lived. As for this rejection of the failed father, there is some reason for believing that John Paul's failure was not merely the result of bad luck but, in the end, of a defect in courage and will. Many men have recovered from situations worse than his; and he did have ability, for long after the failure he was offered a good salary as an adviser for a successful woolen mill. But he had, presumably, become afraid of success, or had fallen in love with failure and with the rigid religiosity in which he had taken refuge. So the son's contempt for the father may well have had deep and complex roots, and the complexity reappears in the son's own ambivalence toward success and toward the American gospel of success.

After the disaster, John Paul, almost penniless, burdened by debt, and with eight children, moved on to Terre Haute, Indiana, where, in 1871, Theodore was born.* From this time on, the family sank deeper into poverty, and John Paul took refuge in his Catholicism, which, as the children grew older and yearned for the colorful life beyond the range of his tyranny, became more and more a matter of sterile, negative discipline.

Fear and contempt were, apparently, the dominant emotions of the children, and certainly of Theodore, if we can judge by his various references to this "thin grasshopper of a man, brooding wearily." Less to the influence of Nietzsche, Machiavelli, and Darwin than to the reaction from the father, the son may have owed his admiration of the ruthless superman whom he celebrated in several novels and sometimes tried, in his personal life, to emulate.

In almost schematic precision, the mother of Theodore was the opposite of John Paul Dreiser—large, maternal, warm-hearted, and instinctual, with no trace of the husband's religiosity and with little conventional moral sense, feeling that people, by and large, were hard-driven by life and might be permitted what small compensatory pleasures could be seized along the way. Dreiser was later to assume, or at least to hope, that she had taken lovers as a refuge from her cheerless lot. She was, as Dreiser says in *Dawn*, one of his autobiographical works, "beyond or behind good and evil." Her morality, in any case, was based on sympathy and pity, and it was from her that Dreiser professed to have learned those qualities that characterize his work. We even have his account of the birth of pity:

> I recall, one hot day, playing on the floor of the front room, and about my mother's knees. (I was always a "mother's child," hanging to her skirts as much as I was permitted until I was seven or eight years old.) I recall her lounging in a white dressing-sacque, a pair of worn slippers on her feet. In my playful peregrinations I came to her feet and began smoothing her toes. I can hear her now. "See poor mother's shoes? Aren't you sorry she

has to wear such worn shoes? See the hole here?" She reached down to show me, and in the wonder and final pity—evoked by the tone of her voice which so long controlled me—I began to examine, growing more and more sorrowful as I did so. And then finally, a sudden, swelling sense of pity that ended in tears.*

Sarah Dreiser tried to hold the family of now ten children together, but it was a losing battle against dire poverty and even the threat of starvation. Once, derelict, they were taken in by the wife of the fire chief of Vincennes, Indiana, only to find that the other rooms over the firehouse served as a place of assignation for local prostitutes; even Sarah Dreiser's flexible code could not quite accept this arrangement. Meanwhile, the boys were getting into trouble. One was jailed for forgery, and eluded his father's plan to make him into a priest by running off with a minstrel troupe, to return later with a fur overcoat and a gold-headed cane, a success as an actor and songwriter under the name of Paul Dresser. He took the miserable family to Evansville, Indiana, where they were installed in a cottage owned by his then mistress, the madam of a brothel, whom he was later to celebrate in the song "My Gal Sal."

Evansville was simply a momentary pause on the downward spiral of the family. It was harder and harder for the father to find work. One sister had already been seduced, by a politician in Terre Haute, and when she became pregnant, was discarded by her lover; that child was stillborn, but when, somewhat later, another sister bore an illegitimate child, it survived and fell to the care of the warm-hearted Sarah Dreiser. Meanwhile, the family was on the move, trying place after place, even Chicago. Late in life, Dreiser was to say that whenever winter came on, he felt, as an echo of those old times of deprivation, "an indefinable and highly oppressive dread," and in *Sister Carrie* he remarks "how firmly the chill hand of winter lays [*sic*] upon the heart." But more than that memory was carried away from those years: a sense of the hard material base of life as the only reality, and the awareness of the injustice of a world that deprives many men of that reality.

During the years of poverty and humiliation, Dreiser was a weak, spindly boy, incompetent at games and cowardly in the rough and tumble of boyhood. But, as his mother's pet, he felt from childhood onward that, somehow, for all his weakness, dreaminess, and ugliness, he was especially chosen to be great, and he records that the refrain of his inner life was "No common man am I." The flashy success of Paul, who now and then burst upon the family to resolve some crisis, seemed to bring the possibility of success within practical range. And two teachers, at different times, sensed some unusual quality underlying the young Dreiser's ignorance and confusion. They confirmed his dream of himself as one of the chosen, and they introduced him to books; and a few years later, when Dreiser had a dead-end job as a stockboy in a hardware store in Chicago, one of them, Mildred Fielding, sought him out, made him give up the job, and out of her own meager savings, sent him, in 1889, to Indiana University.

Mildred Fielding, as far as such a thing can ever be known, made Dreiser the writer. But quite unwittingly, he seems to have done something for her. His clumsiness, ignorance, and yearning seem to have touched some maternal strain in the heart of the schoolmarm; shortly afterwards, she got married and, in the kind of irony that Dreiser the novelist would have understood, died in childbirth.

At the University, Dreiser, poorly prepared, did not do well in his studies, and in his poverty, awkwardness, and conviction of his own ugliness, he felt himself cut off from the gaiety of student life: the confirmed outsider. The next year he went back to Chicago; and as Melville said that his Harvard and Yale were the deck of a whaler, so Dreiser might have said the same of the raw and bustling city into which, still in his teens, he was plunged.

Chicago, in the 1890's, was booming, vital, ambitious, brutal, garish, and corrupt. It was a new city, drawing the immigrants from Europe and the young boys and girls from the farms and small towns of its hinterland. In its physical rawness, in its difference from Boston, New York, and Philadelphia, in which the merciless edges of urban modernity were somewhat blunted by a sense of the past, it suggested a wholly new kind of city, of new energy and new promise. In *Dawn*, looking back on the excitement of that world, Dreiser says:

> Hail, Chicago! First of the daughters of the new world! Strange illusion of hope and happiness that resounded as a paean by your lake of blue! . . . Of what dreams and songs were your walls and ways compounded!

But the city had another, and contradictory, face. If it smiled on the strong or the lucky, it was pitiless to those who failed. Later, in *A Book About Myself*, written when he had taken the full measure of the modern city, Dreiser would describe that other face as "gross and cruel and mechanical." It is the contrast between these two faces —the face of dream and the face of reality—that provides a profound and recurring drama for his work.

In the beginning it was the face of dream that enthralled Dreiser, and even in a series of menial jobs (in one of which he embezzled twenty-five dollars to buy a flashy overcoat) he saw himself as one of "the real rulers of the world." But the youth who saw himself in that role was of unpromising aspect—height six feet one and a half inches, weight one hundred and thirty-seven pounds, with a squint in the left eye, buckteeth, bulbous irregular features, and no compensatory grace of bearing. His education was miserable. He was, he records, "blazing with sex," was a ferocious masturbator, and was consumed by yearnings for wealth, display, and power, and by deep social resentments. One way to become a "ruler" was to marry into the charmed circle, and so in the deep confusion of dreams of sexuality and dreams of power there was the image of the girl who was both sensual and rich. Meanwhile, not finding her, Dreiser used such poor girls as he could find to his purpose, and callously disposed of each when she had served his convenience. He was, in other words, forecasting the story of the hero of his greatest work, *An American Tragedy*.

No rich girls available, Dreiser chose another way to power, and enacted another daydream common to yearning youth: he would be a writer. He was, in that early period, ravished by a column by Eugene Field in *The Daily News*, which, in a humorous and romantic vein, touched on local life, and Dreiser reports that nothing he had ever read (and he was then reading Tolstoy) gave him "quite the same feeling for constructive thought." In other words, the fact of the "realness" of his own Chicago being put into language stirred his imagination more than Tolstoy's magnificent power, and this tells us much about the quality of Dreiser's imagination; it had to be stimulated and fed by the gross and immediate fact. In this context, wandering the slums of Chicago as a bill collector, he began to compose "rhythmic, vaguely formulated word-pictures," which he wrote down and sent to his idol of *The Daily News*. He never had a word of acknowledgment, but he did get a job on a newspaper, and his fate was sealed.

As a newspaper man, he had certain glaring deficiencies. For one thing, he was barely literate. Furthermore, though his imagination fed on fact, he had, as a reporter, a curious contempt for fact—as he was to have in other connections all his life, being, to put it nakedly, a born liar. But these deficiencies did not prevent him from being effective at feature stories about the seamy side of city life. He had the gift of observation when the facts observed had some fundamental relation to human feeling. That is, he had a novelistic and not a reportorial sense of fact.

In this decade Dreiser practiced his craft in Chicago, St. Louis, Toledo, Cleveland, Pittsburgh, and New York. He came to know the underside of the cities—the skid rows, the flophouses, the saloons, and the brothels, where, in fact, he was often a customer. He also came to know the theaters (he sometimes served as a dramatic critic, of sorts), hotels, and flashy nightspots. And he knew, too, the shack towns of the mines in Pennsylvania, and the bloody troubles accompanying the rise of organized labor, and how, in Pittsburgh, the money of the steel-masters controlled all life and all news. So, as he says, he came to ask certain corrosive questions:

> Here then was a part of the work of an omnipotent God, who nevertheless tolerated, apparently, a most industrious devil. Why did he do it? Why did nature, when left to itself, devise such astounding slums and human muck heaps?

In that age of the beginning of modern journalism, when individualism and intellectual curiosity were often a mark of the guild, he met men who read Machiavelli and Nietzsche* and who introduced him to the doctrine of the superman, a doctrine that seemed to justify the ruthlessness of the Robber Barons like Vanderbilt, Carnegie, Rockefeller, and Yerkes, and to justify his own daydream of being a "ruler." He learned, too, about the shocking new scientists and philosophers, such as Darwin, Thomas Huxley, and Herbert Spencer, and his course of reading in them destroyed the last vestige of his religious training, and confirmed him in his contempt for his fanatical and feckless father. But if Machiavelli with his *Prince*, and Spencer and Darwin with their theory of the survival of the fittest, flattered his arrogant daydreams, he also found in the new reading ideas that, paradoxically enough, struck a blow at his egotistical sense of power. Spencer, he says, "showed me that I was a chemical atom in a whirl of unknown forces; the realization clouded my mind."

What was Theodore Dreiser to be? A superman or a chemical atom? The tension of the question was acute. Was he all will, or was he a will-less pawn in a blind process? In either case, what was the moral content of experience? The torturous answer to such questions does not lie in his work. It *is* his work.

Putting some questions aside for the moment, each of the competing views, that of Machiavelli and that of Spencer, gave him an image for one pole of the modern life. In it certain men were merciless predators, monsters of will. But in it, too, a man might feel himself nothing, without personal meaning or value, totally alienated. In the end, even the successful predator might come to this. These competing images lie behind the fiction Dreiser was to write.

We must not assume, however, that, in any simple sense, Dreiser took his ideas from Machiavelli, Spencer, Huxley, and Darwin. Reading them merely gave form to ideas that Dreiser had, year after year, been living into. The reading that did affect him more directly was Balzac, who, in his massive fictions about the life of Paris, gave Dreiser a new sense of the cities that he himself knew. He was not yet a novelist, but Balzac gave him a way to look at his cities, which were not Paris but, even so, were, as he was to say, "something." Balzac gave a new meaning to the lowly reporter's dreary routine of "police and city hall." But Balzac did an even greater service to Dreiser. Dreiser found that Balzac's portraits of "the brooding, seeking, ambitious beginner in life" were, simply, himself. Balzac's fiction made Dreiser see the world; but it also made him see himself in that world. And in the deepest sense, Dreiser's only story was always to be that of himself, "the brooding, seeking, ambitious beginner." But he was to put that story of the young man derived from Balzac into the context derived from Spencer: the dream of glory was dreamed in a world where the dreamer might wake to find that he himself was nothing—only a dream within a dream.

Meanwhile, Dreiser, the ambitious beginner, was astonishingly successful. In that decade he became a magazine editor and a writer of articles for the best-known magazines, with his name listed in *Who's Who*. It did not matter that the articles were hastily worked up, full of errors and plagiarisms, and miserably written; he was making money. He was making enough money, in fact, to get married to a fiancée whom he had long since ceased to desire and with whom matrimony was, as he put it, merely the "pale flame of duty."

No match could have been more inappropriate. Sara White—nicknamed "Jug"—was a pretty, well brought up, conventional woman, somewhat older than the bridegroom—and she had the great misfortune to fall in love with Theodore Dreiser, a man incapable, as he was to say about himself, of loving anybody except, perhaps, the mother whose worn shoes he had once caressed and who was long since dead. Still outraged at old deprivations, haunted by a sense of insufficiency and inferiority, paranoidally suspicious, totally self-centered and brutally selfish, and fearful of impotence, Dreiser had long since found that only a stream of different women could solace his mortally wounded ego. In the end Sara, whose name was, ironically, the same as that of the dead mother, took on the role of a mother rather than that of a wife. She served him, too, by correcting and rewriting his work; for she had been a schoolteacher and knew all about grammar. But she also served his work in another way, as the model for the wife, Angela Blue, in his autobiographical novel *The "Genius,"* and in a more shadowy way as the model for Roberta in *An American Tragedy*.

Under the pressure of a newspaper friend, Arthur Henry, almost on a dare, Dreiser began his first novel. He wrote the words *Sister Carrie* at the top of a sheet of paper, and his career was begun. He had no idea what the novel was to be about, but memory took over. He knew the old yearnings of his sisters and how they had been caught by the glitter of a world beyond them. So we see Carrie, a country girl on a train, on her way to Chicago to hunt work, full of unformulated desires and with no firm moral principles, and see her meet Drouet, a cheap lady-killer in flashy clothes. Dreiser remembered not only his sisters but himself and his own enchantment by Chicago and his own experience as the yearning "beginner," the outsider full of the primal pain of wanting and not having.

Carrie, after a dreary round of job-hunting and then immersion in a dreary job, with the sense of lostness and depersonalization in the swarming city, is easy prey to Drouet. So, later, with her blind aspiration toward something more glittering, she is easy prey to Hurstwood— the manager of a saloon, a "way-up swell place," as

Drouet puts it—who stands at a higher level than Drouet, closer to some mysterious center of power, wealth, and joy that poor Carrie cannot actually conceive but merely senses. And the crucial fact in bringing her to surrender is in this sentence: "Behold, he had ease and comfort, his strength was great, his position high, his clothing rich, and yet he was appealing to her."

But the great Hurstwood is, in a way, a victim, too—merely one of Spencer's chemical atoms. Even when Hurstwood takes ten thousand dollars from the safe of his employers (an episode based on the fact that the lover of one of Dreiser's sisters had stolen from his employer and fled with the girl), the event is, in a sense, an accident, a trap baited by fate into which Hurstwood falls. He is holding the money in his hand, debating the theft, when the lock of the safe clicks. Had he pushed the door? He does not know. In this brilliant moral and psychological study, what is the nature of Hurstwood's guilt? Is the slamming of the door an accident or an alibi, a trap of fate or a masking of the unconscious decision to steal?

As Richard Lehan points out in his valuable study, *Theodore Dreiser: His World and His Novels,* Dreiser kept revising this scene, apparently realizing that it was central to his conception, and the revision progressed from a scene of explicitly debated temptation toward one of moral ambiguity; the movement is from a decision to steal, which, in the first version, precedes the click of the lock, to the final version in which the "accident" seems to account for the act. While part of the general revision of the novel was to emphasize the nature of what seems to be "chance" in human life, another impulse emerges—the growing insistence, not on the role of "chance" in the objective world, but on the apparently indeterminate elements in the inner life of men. In fact, the main direction of the revision was to deepen the characters of both Carrie and Hurstwood, to modify the conception from that of the mere adventuress and the mere seducer, to increase the shadowy ambiguity in the growth of motive and the forming of decision. At the same time, there is a movement toward a sense of logic behind the ambiguity, but a logic which undercuts all moralistic debate—a logic that grinds on its relentless way in the unconscious levels of life.

For instance, as a structural, as well as thematic, parallel with the scene of Hurstwood, we have the scene when Hurstwood first calls on Carrie in Drouet's absence, a scene in which we find the same moral ambiguity. At the end of the call, which has been, in a literal sense, innocent enough, Hurstwood tries to implicate Carrie in an unspecified guilt by pledging her to secrecy. She "doubtfully" replies: "I can't promise." But as soon as Hurstwood is gone, we find this passage:

> She undid her broad lace collar before the mirror and unfastened her pretty alligator belt which she had recently bought.
> "I'm getting terrible," she said, honestly affected by a feeling of trouble and shame. "I don't seem to do anything right."
> She unloosed her hair after a time and let it hang in loose brown waves. Her mind was going over the events of the evening. "I don't know," she murmured at last, "what I can do."

At this point, Carrie has done nothing "terrible." The "terrible" unspecified thing lies in the future, but all the time, while she is experiencing the "feeling of trouble and shame," she is removing the finery bought with Drouet's money, and releasing her hair as though preparing to go to bed—with Hurstwood. Let us notice, too, that she is doing all this while staring, uncomprehendingly, at the image of the incomprehensible self there in the mirror—the self that will pursue its own fated way in spite of anything that she "can do."

Nothing is specified, nothing is clear, but how clearly and deeply we intuit in this little drama the nature of the complex process working itself out. Over and over again in his fiction Dreiser develops such moments of psychological depth. And in *An American Tragedy*, in Clyde at the death of Roberta, we find his masterpiece of psychological analysis.

It can reasonably be held that the sense of moral ambiguity is central for *Sister Carrie*, as it is central for *An American Tragedy*. In one perspective, the whole story of Carrie and her lovers is a study of the mechanical process of success and failure—a process that to Dreiser appears as unrelated to morality as a chemical experiment. By inscrutable laws, some fall, some rise. Hurstwood sinks to ruin, Carrie rises to be a theatrical star, but success and failure are both aspects of a morally neutral process.

Sex, love, appetite, loyalty—all feelings seem to shrivel to meaninglessness before the cold objective law of success and failure. Stage by stage we observe Hurstwood on the "road downward" that "has but few landings and level places," and stage by stage, we see the changes in Carrie's attitude and behavior toward Hurstwood. From the first moment of boredom she passes to indifference, then to disgust, then to contempt and cruelty, and then to a coldly mechanical act of desertion, and all, in the end, passes into a blank forgetfulness. In other words, Hurstwood is, bit by bit, robbed of reality. Failure is a kind of death that precedes the mortal death, and the mortal death will be, ironically enough, merely the shadow of the "spiritual" death. Several years earlier, in the winter of 1896–97, in an editorial in his first magazine, *Ev'ry Month*, Dreiser commented on the current money panic and the suffering entailed by it: "In this world generally failure opens wide the gates to mortal onslaught, and the invariable result is death."* From this brutal editorial, with its underlying theme of the survival of the fittest and the idea of the "psychosomatic" relation between the hard world of economic competition and the physiological fate, we find a dramatic projection in poor Hurstwood; especially in the night scene in which Hurstwood, having decided to commit suicide, goes past the theater to take a last look at Carrie's name in "incandescent fire," and continuing on his way, slips and falls in the snow and slush outside the splendor of the Waldorf, where Carrie now lives. But long since, in the long process of the decay of their relation, both Carrie and Hurstwood have recognized the law of their condition, and both, in a deep unformulated sense, accept it.

The law of success and failure has, indeed, been long since demonstrated in Carrie's desertion of her kin for Drouet, and of Drouet for Hurstwood. The law is reasserted, toward the end of the novel, when Drouet, still the glossy skirt-chaser and now somewhat risen in the world, appears in New York and thinks he may recapture Carrie; but she is beyond him, his success is not in her dimension. By the law of success and failure, there is no place for him in her scheme of things.

From the opening of the novel Carrie has, in fact, been instinctively aware of the mechanism of success. Dreiser calls her a "little soldier of fortune," and that is literally what she is, an adventuress with an instinctive eye to the main chance, as undistracted by sex, or love, as by moral scruples. Furthermore, she instinctively reads the symbols of the world of success, and the first symbol is Drouet's clothes; in the end she is seduced, not by his manly qualities, but by the cut of his coat. Commenting on this, Dreiser says: "A woman should some day write the complete philosophy of clothes. No matter how young, it is one of the things she wholly comprehends." It was, too, one of the things the young Dreiser had comprehended: he had stolen twenty-five dollars for a coat that, long before he had attained any success, would serve as a symbol of success.

In Carrie's story Dreiser subtly develops the way in which commitment to what he would call "material" success could absorb all other aspects of life. The groundwork of this process, as we have remarked above, is laid by Drouet's clothes; and the next stage in the process occurs when, after her early struggle in Chicago, she again encounters Drouet, who takes her to dinner and gives her money. With her fingers touching the "soft, green handsome ten-dollar bills" (notice how the description endows the symbols, i.e., the bills, with intrinsic charm), she suddenly feels that she likes Drouet, and could continue to like him "ever so much."* And she does continue to like him until she meets Hurstwood, who opens her eyes to new vistas. But with Hurstwood, as with Drouet, what is remarkable is the coldness—the mechanical quality—of the sexual relation. On this point, at the moment of her marriage to Hurstwood, Dreiser is quite specific: "There was no great passion in her, but the drift of things and this man's proximity created a semblance of affection." It is one of the moments of beautiful precision in Dreiser's writing. "Drift of things" —"proximity"—"semblance": could it be better, more succinctly, put?

Here we may remember that, late in life, Dreiser, after his own bitter struggle for success and his years of compulsive promiscuity, could say that he had never loved anybody except perhaps his mother, that he had loved women merely in the abstract; that is, he had seen women as "mechanisms" for a certain pleasure, not as persons. As Flaubert is reported, perhaps erroneously, to have said of his great heroine Madame Bovary, that she was himself, so Dreiser, the soldier of fortune incapable of love, might have said, "Caroline Meeber, *c'est moi.*" She is the first of the shadow-selves about whom Dreiser wrote: the first of the images that embodied his own yearning and struggle, and that, at the same time, endured the cold scalpel-edge of psychological analysis and suffered that vengeance for the outrage Dreiser himself had done to his own secret and incorrigible moral sense.

The feelings of sex, love, and affection do not prevail against the cold mechanism of success and failure that the story of Carrie delineates, but the novel is shot through with, even sustained and given life by, other feelings. There is the pathos of yearning, of wanting and not having, and the slow, grinding anguish of failure. The decline of Hurstwood—one of the great narrative sequences in American fiction—is rendered with almost intolerable imaginative involvement. It is as though Dreiser, even as he, the rising young journalist, began to taste success, became hagridden with the fear of failure; so, in his neurotically superstitious nature, he was driven to expiate the "crime" of success by realizing imaginatively all the pangs of failure and, by this expiation, to try to pay in advance for success.* Thus the very compassion in the novel may have a deep aspect of self-reference, and the poignancy may actually be the result of that self-reference.

There is, however, another range of feeling in the novel, also deeply related to Dreiser's own compulsive drive for success. Along with this drive there was—as there often is—a paradoxical criticism of success, even a rejection of it, a conviction that success is bound to be empty and meaningless, an unformulated awareness that success is sought so desperately only as a compensation for some fundamental and irremediable deprivation or failure, and that no success can, in the end, ever be a surrogate for what has been denied. So we find Dreiser, even in the full tide of his drive for success, suffering the shock of the encounter with Herbert Spencer, and saying of himself:

Up to this time there had been a blazing and un-checked desire to get on, the feeling that in doing so we did get somewhere; now in its place was the definite con-viction that spiritually one got nowhere. . . .

There is, then, a pathos of success as well as of failure, and as Hurstwood exemplifies one, so Carrie exemplifies the other—and this contrast provides, struc-turally, the poles of the action. As Hurstwood has been doomed to failure, so Carrie has been doomed to success, and at the end we see her in the apartment at the Waldorf:

Oh, Carrie, Carrie! Oh, blind strivings of the human heart! Onward, onward, it saith, and where beauty leads, there it follows. Whether it be the tinkle of a lone sheep bell o'er some quiet landscape, or the glimmer of beauty in sylvan places, or the show of soul in some passing eye, the heart knows and makes answer, following. It is when the feet weary and hope seems in vain that the heart-aches and the longings arise. Know, then, that for you is neither surfeit nor content. In your rocking-chair, by your window dreaming, shall you long alone. In your rocking-chair, by your window, shall you dream such happiness as you may never feel.

Carrie has everything, and she has nothing, and the rocking chair—motion without progress, life spent in mere repetition, a hypnotic dream without content—is a perfect image of the success that "got nowhere."* It is the image of the pathos of success—and to sit rocking by the hour was one of Dreiser's own characteristic habits. To sit rocking while over and over again he would fold and unfold a handkerchief. The paradox of success con-tinued, in various forms, to haunt Dreiser, as in *A Gallery of Women*, where, in reference to "Regina C——," he says of ambitious women that they draw "a certain kind of success or disaster about as plants draw a certain kind of insect." Success and disaster, success and failure—these can be convertible terms in the logic of life.

In *The Dream of Success*, Kenneth Lynn offers a very interesting account of the scene of Carrie in her chair. He notes a psychoanalytic account of the "gold digger" that describes the type as "invariably severely neurotic . . . capable of achieving their conscious aims temporarily, only to find themselves depressed, dissatisfied, bored." But he adds a sociological dimension to the scene in the Waldorf, for which, he says, Dreiser gives a clue in the fact that Carrie, sitting in her rocking chair, is yawning over Balzac's *Père Goriot*. Dreiser, as I have already said, had, only a few years earlier, discovered Balzac and recognized in his ambitious, success-mad young men the picture of himself, and de Rastignac, the hero of this novel, is a perfect exemplar of that cold-hearted breed. It would be a typical instance of that subtlety (for which Dreiser is so rarely praised) for him to put *Père Goriot* on Carrie's knee, as a way of identifying himself (consciously or unconsciously) with her, and a way of confessing, in the same fact, the emptiness of his own values, and, under the guise of pity for her, expressing a pity for himself as the ultimate victim. And connected with this self-pity outwardly directed, we may recall that when Dreiser saw the scene of the death cell in the stage version of *An American Tragedy*, tears came to his eyes as he murmured: "The poor boy, the poor boy! What a shame." But we may recall, too, the scene in that novel when Clyde Griffiths, finding his sister abandoned and pregnant, experiences, like circles widening out from the stone dropped into a pool, the pity for her, then for their mother, and then for the world; and finally, from under the guise of those objective forms of pity, the pity for himself bursts out, for he, too, is trapped in the mess.

Kenneth Lynn, however, is concerned to make a point somewhat different from Dreiser's identification with Carrie and the relation of pity and self-pity. He would emphasize the sociological aspect of the scene; referring to Alexis de Tocqueville, who, in *Democracy in America*, remarked that the interest of life to Americans consists in anticipated success, Lynn goes on to say that de Rastignac would not be bored as Carrie is, for in a society of birth and status like that of France the challenges to the *arriviste* remain infinite, while in a plutocracy, once the symbols of conspicuous consumption are achieved, there are no other worlds to conquer.

The observations of Lynn offer a valuable comparison, but it is one made by him, not by Dreiser. When Dreiser read Balzac, he saw a likeness, not a difference. For one thing, he was looking at the psychology of the deprived and ambitious young soldier of fortune and not at the society that offered the objects of his ambition. For another thing, even if he had had such an interest, nothing in his education, experience, or cast of mind would have equipped him to pursue it fruitfully. He did not even understand the complexities of American society except at the level at which he did treat it. Dreiser is as far from Henry James as Nigger Jim and Huck Finn on their raft are from Prince Amerigo, or the White Whale from Edith Wharton herself. Dreiser was not, and could not have been, a novelist of manners. He was, quite literally, a novelist of the metaphysics of society—of, specifically, the new plutocratic society of the Gilded Age. And this meant that he was, too, the anatomist of the guilt involved in the characteristic ambition of that age as well as the poet of the pathos of success.

This theme of Dreiser's, it may be added, lies at a different and deeper level from that of the novel of manners. Such a theme may, however, be sometimes found behind the façade of the novel of manners; for instance, Proust's *A la recherche du temps perdu* is a masterwork in the genre of manners, but its final power comes from the unmasking of the reality of the world Marcel had dreamed of entering and from his own re-definition of reality. Even if it is enacted in a world infinitely more complex than that of Carrie, the story of Marcel is similar to hers. Each, of course, has assaulted a "walled city," as Dreiser puts it, each has breached the wall, and each has entered to find a reality far different from what had been dreamed. If Marcel is not bored, it is not because the complexity of his world offers infinite challenge for the conquest of new forms of status. What challenges him is not in the sociological dimension; it is to find a new form of reality in the aesthetic dimension, in the telling of the tale. The point is that Proust recognizes the significance of that dimension, and has faith in it because he can distinguish it from the sociological.

And this distinction is precisely what Dreiser could never quite make. He was a powerful artist, but his artistic ambition was painfully intermingled with his ambition for money and fine clothes; in fact, he often saw his work as a mere instrument to satisfy his grossest aspirations. It is only natural, then, that success of the artist should, to him, seem as fragile and infected as that of Cowperwood, the hero of *The Financier*, or any Robber Baron. Let us remember that it is as an "artist" that Carrie succeeds, and it is an artist who, in the apartment in the Waldorf, sits in the rocking chair that goes nowhere. But Carrie is not merely "artist," she is also "artist as gold digger," and so, may we ask, does this image represent another level of self-scrutiny on the part of Dreiser—who had his own rocking chair?

When Dreiser wrote *Sister Carrie*, he had not yet breached the "walled city," he had merely invested the outworks. The great test yet lay before him. If he was, as he says of Carrie, full of "wild dreams of some vague, far-off supremacy," he, as the "mother's child" with the sense of omnipotence and of being chosen by fate that Freud attributes to one in that position, still had enough of his father's religiosity and bitter ascetic morality, and enough superstitious anxiety, to be fearful, as I have suggested, of his very dreams of conquest. More important, he had enough imagination to leap forward to the moment of fulfilling conquest, and ask himself, "What will I have when I have it?" *Sister Carrie* appears as the projection of his own secret conflict and self-scrutiny; perhaps not the projection of them, but the means by which he discovered them at all. It may well be, that is, that he could discover them only when they were embodied in Caroline Meeber and not in Theodore Dreiser.

I have been speaking as though *Sister Carrie* were important primarily as a historical and social document and as a record of the psychology of Dreiser. But it is more than a document, it is a vivid and absorbing work of art. In dealing with a novel, the most obvious question is what kind of material the author has thought worth his treating, what kind of world stimulates his imagination. For Dreiser this was the world he lived in—and the world he was—and by accepting as fully as possible this limitation, he enlarged, willy-nilly, by a kind of historical accident if you will, the range of American literature. The same kind of compulsive veracity (so strangely mixed with his compulsive lying) that made him record such details of his own life as masturbation and theft, made him struggle to convert into fiction the substances of experience at both the personal and social levels that had not been earlier absorbed.

The kind of realism that is associated with William Dean Howells had little relation to the depths that Dreiser inhabited, and when Howells, the editor of the sacrosanct *Atlantic Monthly* and dean of American letters, encountered Dreiser shortly after the publication of his first novel, he felt compelled, according to a report that, if not literally, is spiritually true, to remark: "You know, I don't like *Sister Carrie*." Even though his eyes had long since been unsealed by Tolstoy to the degradation and pain of the poor and to the brutality of power in the modern world, even though he had courageously declared himself on the affair of the Haymarket bombing, Howells, however sympathetic and anguished he might be, still remained the outsider to that grim world that was Dreiser's natural home. And even if Frank Norris had shocked the country with the realism of *McTeague*, he had, in the end, gratified the moral sense of America by converting the novel of greed and violence into a cautionary fable.

Sister Carrie was different from anything by Howells or Norris. What was shocking here was not only Dreiser's unashamed willingness to identify himself with morally undifferentiated experience or his failure to punish vice and reward virtue in his fiction, but the implication that vice and virtue might, in themselves, be mere accidents, mere irrelevances in the process of human life, and that the world was a great machine, morally indifferent. Ultimately, what shocked the world in Dreiser's work was not so much the things that he presented as the fact that he himself was not shocked by them. The situation was similar to that of Dreiser's hero Machiavelli, who shocked his world not by unveiling the nakedness of power (the world knew all about that), but by regarding it with a moral detachment, by trying to delineate a physics, even a metaphysics, of power.

The world that an author accepts is more than material, it is the great overarching and undergirding image of the author's deepest concerns; and all his particular fictions merely develop what is implicit in that great germ image. The world thus rendered—that is, the material of a novel —cannot, in the end, be distinguished, except by an act of abstraction, from the quality of the rendering. It is only by some deep coherence of the "rendered" and the "rendering" that a novel achieves the total, inner vibrance that guarantees permanence. We shall come later to the general question of Dreiser's art, but now we may remark that *Sister Carrie* introduced a novelty of method as well as of material and attitude; and the method was so spontaneously generated out of the material and attitude that it is scarcely to be recognized as a method at all, merely as a natural event.

At first glance, *Sister Carrie* seems to be a loose chronicle, the kind of narrative furthest removed from the well-made novel of a carefully wrought plot with logical interrelations and an increasing intensity that moves to a summarizing climax. Here, drift and accident are the obvious "realistic" elements, but Dreiser, even in violating the logic of the well-made plot, has developed a deeper thematic logic, with psychological grounding, to give both thrust and structure to the work. If we analyze the psychological and thematic significance of the key elements in Carrie's career, from the first meeting with Drouet to the scene of the rocking chair and *Père Goriot*, we find that we have here a very compelling drive and a coherent structure: Carrie's movement upward, like Hurstwood's movement downward, involves its characteristic suspense, and at the same time the movement is marked by stages that convert chronological flow into closely articulated structure. The two movements are in structural counterpoint, each being enriched and reinforced by ironic parallels and contrasts in the other, these parallels and contrasts constituting a dialectical progression, a development of the thematic logic. Further, the appearance of Drouet at the beginning and at the end serves to bracket the main action in a simple structural fashion; but, further, Drouet serves a deeper purpose, offering a counterpoint to both lives, to the high success of Carrie and the ruin of Hurstwood. He, Drouet, is the casual by-product, the drifter on the tide of things, significant in his insignificance, pitiful in his psychological and animal complacencies. To sum up, the apparently casual structure of mere chronicle is set against a very firm and complex structure of thematic contrast and parallelism, and in the tension between these two principles of structure—the narrative and the thematic—the vital rhythm of the novel is defined.

Good fortune may come in many guises, and one is that of ill-fortune. *Sister Carrie* was a resounding failure. Frank Norris, who was working at Doubleday, Page and Company, had fallen in love with *Sister Carrie* at first sight, had accepted it for publication, and had used all his prestige as a brilliantly successful novelist to persuade others in the firm of its merit. But when Mrs. Doubleday read the book, its doom was sealed. The firm tried to renege on the contract, but Dreiser, within his legal rights, insisted on publication. The book sold only four hundred fifty-six copies, and netted the author only sixty-eight dollars and forty cents.

If the veracity that shines in Dreiser's fiction is found only infrequently in his reporting, it is scandalously rare in certain personal records. In his characteristic imaginings, the failure of *Sister Carrie* was the result of a deliberate conspiracy, inspired by Mrs. Doubleday, to stay within the letter of the contract and yet suppress the book. The publishers, in fact, very carefully fulfilled the letter of the contract, distributed review copies, and were prompt in handling orders. But the romantic tale of high-handed and purblind abuse that Dreiser scattered far and wide, became the generally accepted version. The public did not buy *Sister Carrie,* but they did buy Dreiser's story about why they did not buy *Sister Carrie.* Out of his failure, Dreiser created his success. *Sister Carrie* became a cause célèbre. It became a battle cry of the young, and a symbol of the new freedom, and when, in 1901, the book appeared in England, the gratifying recognition it received in reputable quarters did something to salve the author's wounded vanity and laid the basis for the novel's future success in America.

Critical success was, however, all the book achieved in England. The royalties amounted to only a little over one hundred dollars, and Dreiser fell into a period of frightful depression. His chronic anxiety about money became acute. He found it difficult to write or place articles. He did have a small advance against the projected *Jennie Gerhardt,* but he could not get on with it. A period of wandering ensued. Relations with his wife Jug went from bad to worse, and finally he sent her back to her family and, almost penniless, returned to New York. He was near starvation, and felt himself verging toward insanity or suicide, and all the terrors of failure that had been projected into Hurstwood were now his own fate. He was too proud to appeal to relatives, above all to

Paul, for whom his admiration was tangled with jealousy and with whom he had quarreled.

But Paul, by a chance encounter, found him, and put him on a "health farm" to rebuild his strength and morale. When Dreiser recovered, he took a job at manual labor with the New York Central Railroad, but the fits of depression were recurrent, and he had to struggle to regain his sense of "individuality," and his "old belief in the reality of things." By the end of 1904, however, he was ready to leave the job on the railroad and try to pick up his ruined career.

Within a short time Dreiser was successful beyond his wildest dreams, not as a writer but as a magazine editor, first for pulp publications and later as top editor of the rich Butterick group, the *Delineator*, the *New Idea Woman's Magazine* and the *Designer*. These were "women's magazines," devoted to fashion, household concerns, child-rearing, and society, with a smattering of stories and articles; but all this was merely bait—the real function of the Butterick publications was to sell dress patterns.

Out of the years of breakdown, Dreiser had emerged with an even stronger will to success—success interpreted in the crassest terms—and with a readiness to pay any price for it. To him Darwinism had meant the law of the jungle, and already in an editorial in one of his pulp magazines, he had written, "Success is what counts in the world, and it is little matter how success is won." To him the survival of the fittest meant to disregard "conceptions of art or ethics" and to see "the world as it actually is." Onto the jungle law of force Dreiser had thus grafted Machiavelli's axiom of realism. With Machiavelli, he recognized, too, that not only the strength of the lion but the cunning of the fox may be necessary to achieve success, and in this vein he wrote a statement of the editorial policy for his best-known magazine:

> The *Delineator's* message is human betterment. Its appeal is to the one great harmonizing force of humanity —womanhood. To sustain it, to broaden it, to refine it, to inspire it, is our aim. Our theme is one that a woman may carry into her house, her church and her social affairs—the theme of the ready smile, the theme of the ungrudged helping hand.

He added that the purpose of the *Delineator* was to strengthen every woman "in her moral fight for righteousness in the world."

Dreiser was never a man notable for humor, certainly not for self-humor, but even he must have found some amusement, however grim, in the spectacle of the author of *Sister Carrie*, the exponent of social Darwinism, the hater of religion, the hardened adulterer and compulsive skirt-chaser, thus dedicating himself to help every woman "in her moral fight for righteousness." But in the end, the humor was to be double-edged. He was to lose the best job he ever held because, not content with the rotating harem that, in his new prosperity, he had gathered, he undertook to seduce the seventeen-year-old daughter of a female member of his staff.

Meanwhile, however, Dreiser drove furiously for his success. He assembled able subordinates. He could be brutal when occasion demanded. He knew how to collect and sometimes debauch talent, including the young H. L. Mencken, who—though the fact beggars belief—ghosted

a series of articles on the care and feeding of babies, and
Sinclair Lewis, who wrote a poem that begins:

> When I stay out and slide till late
> I hear my Nursey scold:
> "O R-r-obin! You come right straight!
> You'll catch a death of cold!"

Dreiser gagged at nothing: not the Tiny Wren Club
organized to sell patterns for doll clothes, articles on the
"joys of motherhood," the Child Rescue Campaign, the
Santa Claus Association, the Boy Knights of the Round
Table, the campaign against the Teddy Bear undertaken
because bears, unlike dolls, don't need dress patterns
("Bring your babies back to dollies or you will have
weaned the grown-ups of the future from the babies that
will never be"). He did not even gag at the fiction selected in strict conformity with his editorial instruc-
tions: "We like sentiment, we like humor, we like
realism, but it must be tinged with sufficient idealism
to make it all of a truly uplifting character. . . . We
cannot admit stories which deal with false or immoral
relations. . . . The finer side of things—the idealistic—
is the answer for us."

Dreiser's frenetic energy spilled beyond the office of
the Butterick publications. He was carrying on clandes-
tine publishing operations, one for books, one for a
magazine, with some dabbling in real estate in the East
and apple-growing in the West. And, too, there was his
courtship of the young Thelma Cudlipp, exciting, time-
consuming, and unrewarded. In the background of all
these projects there was the novel *Jennie Gerhardt*
waiting to be finished.

Luck intervened to get it finished—good luck again in the guise of ill. In October 1910, thanks to the outraged mother of the girl he was trying to seduce, Dreiser was fired, without warning. Now he had the time to get on with the novel, and his creative will was fueled by the fact that a few years earlier *Sister Carrie* had been reissued and had found a respectful press. Now separated from Jug, and with the young girl snatched off to England, Dreiser set seriously to work. Seated at a desk made from the old rosewood piano that had belonged to his now dead brother Paul and that could evoke that early vision of success and all the tangle of envy, admiration, and resentment associated with it, he drove himself mercilessly. The book was finished in January 1911. It was published the following October, a year almost to the day after he had been fired.

Dreiser had begun *Jennie Gerhardt* as early as December 1900 or January 1901—that is, almost immediately after finishing *Sister Carrie*—and the new novel was, in a deep and complex way, parallel to the old. Like *Sister Carrie*, it echoes the story of the Dreiser family, in which two daughters had borne illegitimate children. Jennie, like Carrie, comes from a poor family and, like Carrie, is seduced by a man from the world of wealth and privilege. It would seem that Dreiser had set out, in much the same spirit as before, to work the same family materials and repeat the characteristic story of a "little soldier of fortune." In work done between the beginning and 1904, when he laid the project aside, there is, as Richard Lehan points out, little hint of the theme of the final version. In the earlier version there is no emphasis on Jennie's innocence, maidenly shyness, and complexity of feeling, and the commercial aspect of the transaction is clear. In the same spirit, Senator Brander is presented as the conscious and experienced seducer, and Lester Kane is described as having a "Machiavellian manner" when he exploits Jennie's sense of consideration for her mother to make her yield to him.

As Dreiser had revised *Sister Carrie* to give greater psychological subtlety and to emphasize the role of the unconscious in the development of the heroine, so when he resumed work on *Jennie Gerhardt* in 1910, he complicated not only her character, but those of her lovers, and even more radically changed direct parallels with *Sister Carrie* to parallels by contrast, making this novel a sort of mirror-image of *Sister Carrie*. If Dreiser is now dealing with the old family material and his old exploration of his own nature, he is doing so in order to seek, consciously or unconsciously, new and contradictory possibilities of meaning.

For example, though Jennie, like Carrie, enters the world of wealth by seduction, she, unlike Carrie, is not seduced by the glitter of wealth. She is no gold digger, she is capable of love. To approach Dreiser's meaning from another angle, we may point out that the men who are drawn to Jennie—the middle-aged Senator Brander and the rich young man Lester Kane—are in significant contrast to Drouet and Hurstwood. Brander and Kane are drawn by some intuition of Jennie's capacity for sympathy, unselfishness, and love. Though Jennie is so far beneath him in the social scale, Senator Brander, when Jennie bears his child, is happily preparing to marry her and is only prevented by death; and later Lester Kane, even after he knows the paternity of the child, feels a deep satisfaction in the day-to-day life with Jennie. Sexuality is the appeal offered by the cold-hearted Carrie, but sexuality is only a component of the appeal offered by Jennie; the "capacity for deep feeling" is what Senator Brander finds in the girl Jennie, a feeling that colors her total response to and appreciation of life, and that is what Lester Kane finds too. In other words, the Senator and Lester, unlike Drouet and Hurst-wood, who are totally fulfilled in the world of success, repudiate its values, and find values in Jennie that the practical world scorns.

This is not to say that Jennie is unaware of the "material" base of life. She knows as only the poor can know, and as Dreiser knew, the value of money, but she can translate that value into other values—into what money can mean for the good of those she loves, her mother, her brothers and sisters, and even her father, for whom, in spite of his tyrannical and bigoted nature, she has feeling. In the end, when Robert Kane, Lester's "successful" and conventional brother, gives him the choice of marrying Jennie, with a modest guaranteed income, or leaving her, again with a guarantee of security for her, to resume his place in the world, it is Jennie who forces the issue. What is remarkable is that Dreiser can portray her generosities without making her into a saccharine saint. She makes her renunciation with full awareness of the cost to her, but with no masochistic satisfactions, self-pity, or self-righteousness;

Dreiser conveys this by offering such acts as a natural reflex of her full value, not isolated, we might say, as individual moral decisions.

There is another factor to be considered here. In *Sister Carrie* I have referred to the recognition of the merciless "natural" law of success and failure. Here, in a different context and with a different tonality, Dreiser shows that Jennie also recognizes in the workings of society such a law, or doom, that can contravene love, devotion, and justice. In one perspective, her renunciation is a recognition of this law. Jennie's final renunciation is, in fact, early prepared for when, in Egypt, Jennie and Lester encounter his old flame. Lester and the old flame belong, Jennie painfully recognizes, to a world where she can never come; and this objective recognition works to disinfect her later renunciation of sentimentality. We might even go so far as to say that her renunciation is little more than a recognition of what would happen anyway: that somehow choice in the matter would be, for Lester, only an illusion in the face of the great machine of society and its ineluctable logic.

At this point it is instructive to recall that in the first version of the novel, the end was a happy marriage for Lester and Jennie, with Jennie's daughter well and happy too. We have no way of knowing whether Dreiser had become the victim of his own editorials for the *Delineator* or whether, as one of his friends suggested, he had tacked on the happy and moral ending to placate the reviewers who had attacked *Sister Carrie;* but in any case, Dreiser soon realized that the happy ending violated the logic of his material and its pervasive feeling.

So Lester obeys Jennie and marries the appropriate and doting wife, and sinks into a life of expensively coddled torpor, the life of unreality from which he had fled to Jennie. Jennie is, however, called to visit him on his deathbed, and in a scene of restraint and masterfully rendered emotional implications, the meaning of their relation is summarized. After his death, Jennie, veiled, is at the railroad station to see the casket loaded on the baggage car to be carried back to Cleveland; she has long since lost her daughter, but now lives on, finding solace in two adopted children and in her overflowing sense of sympathetic fulfillment in life.

When Dreiser wrote this new ending, he was not only following the logic of his material and the pervasive feeling of the work, he was also clarifying the thematic line. As *Sister Carrie* tells a sardonic tale of the pitilessly blank world dominated by the two obsessions of success and failure, so the story of Jennie is concerned with the discovery of meaning beyond that world. Negatively, both the Senator and Lester are, as we have seen, disillusioned men drawn to Jennie's unspoken promise of meaningfulness in life. Positively, this meaningfulness must be affirmed outside of the world of success; that is, it must be affirmed as a value discovered in the fact of failure—at Lester's deathbed and in the life of Jennie afterwards. It is an ideal value that must be created outside the concerns of practicality, in the individual's intuition of life as a human community of sympathy and compassion. So, in this last movement of the novel we find both a thematic and structural fulfillment.

Jennie Gerhardt is, in one sense, the most personal of Dreiser's novels. Here the man who was obsessed with sexuality, haunted by the fear of impotence, and unable to regard a woman as other than an anatomical convenience or to respect one as a person, the man who, by his own admission, was incapable of love, set out to write a novel about the definition of love. Here the man who is obsessed with success, haunted by the fear of failure and an irremediable anxiety about money, hagridden by vanity, and tortured by suspicion, set out to write a novel about an inner peace achieved, outside the world of success and failure, by a triumph of spirit. In other words, the deepest drama of the novel is the confrontation of the self of the novelist and the anti-self; and herein lies the deep paradox of the novel. If Jennie first appears as the outsider, the yearner, in the end she is the insider, secure in a charmed place to which the inhabitants of the loud world cannot penetrate. If Dreiser is characteristically the poet of the poor and deprived who yearn to enter the glittering world, in this novel he reverses his role to become another and more deprived kind of outsider, and the deep yearning that permeates the novel is that of the worldling who can dream the secret of peace but cannot enter where it dwells.

In a more specific way, this novel is intensely personal. The image of Dreiser's mother stands behind Jennie's mother, but even more significantly, she stands behind Jennie herself; for Jennie may be taken as the embodiment of the qualities that Dreiser celebrated in his mother and that, somehow, he could never find elsewhere. In a novel he could transfer those qualities to a young woman admirably designed for deep and abiding love—the kind of woman that Dreiser, in the real world, could never find, or could not recognize. And in this connection, we must wonder with what irony, if any, Dreiser regarded the fact that his much-abused wife, now living with him again, was sweating away to correct his bad grammar in the manuscript of *Jennie Gerhardt,* and, more importantly, to cut the elephantine composition down to a marketable size.

We may also wonder with what irony poor Jug regarded the task.

Dreiser's father comes into *Jennie Gerhardt* with scarcely less significance than the mother. Mr. Gerhardt is a faithful picture of him, bigoted, harsh, tyrannical, unsympathetic, lost, and defeated; but one of the most touching things in the novel is the forgiveness that Jennie shows such a father, and the love with which she accepts him is, in the end, a redemption for him. In the real world Dreiser remained unrelenting toward his own father. The only forgiveness and purgation he could attain were in the dream that is fiction.

Jennie Gerhardt, in spite of prolixity and the frequent grossness of the writing, received considerable acclaim. Mencken, for instance, pronounced it the best American novel, "with the Himalayan exception of *Huck Finn.*" But the sales were a distinct disappointment. Dreiser, in his role of "artist as gold digger," was soon confiding to Mencken that if, after three more books, there was "no money in the game," he would quit and go back to editing. He had two more novels on the way and, he said, expected to do them in six months each. That is, in one half of his deeply cleft being, Dreiser regarded his fiction as little more than a sort of hackwork, to be knocked off as rapidly as possible, not devotedly lived into, an occupation to be justified merely on the grounds of financial success.

The books that Dreiser already had under way illustrated another and even deeper cleft in his nature. *Sister Carrie*, delineating the blankness of the world obsessed with success and failure, and *Jennie Gerhardt*, affirming a spiritual meaning beyond that world, can be thought of as written under the aegis of the mother, as the negative and positive aspects of an inspiration derived from her. But the two books that Dreiser now had in mind, *The "Genius"* and *The Financier*, affirming the values of the practical world and advertising the grandeur of the superman, can be thought of as written under the aegis of the father. That is, in revulsion from, in contempt of, the bigoted, sex-hating failure that was John Paul Dreiser, the son now proceeded to celebrate untrammeled sexuality and the ruthless pursuit of success; and here he projects the cherished image of himself as conqueror, with echoes of Balzac, Spencer, and Darwin and of the old incantation, "No common man am I."

*T*he *"Genius"* was a thinly disguised version of Dreiser's ambitious career, his marriage, his promiscuous love affairs, of the passion he had for Thelma Cudlipp, and the revenge visited upon him by her mother. Though still married, and living with his wife, Dreiser made the new novel a justification of the freedom the "genius" sought from the restricting conventionality and stupidity of a small-town girl, and in the process gave a cruelly embarrassing account of the intimate details of his relationship to Jug, from the early infatuation through the dreary sense of obligation that led to marriage, on through the long sequel of betrayals and reconciliations. This sadistic exercise was performed, literally, in the daily presence of Jug. Under her unwitting gaze, Dreiser was contriving a time bomb to explode someday and settle the hash of Sara White, the silly prig from a farm in Missouri, who hadn't been willing to go to bed with him until she had the ring on.

He was going to settle the hash of Thelma Cudlipp, too, whom in real life he called Flowerface and who in fiction retains that name. At the end of the novel Eugene Witla, the "genius" who in the first version had been a newspaperman but is now wearing the thin disguise of a painter, has become, in spite of the mother of Flowerface, successful and famous. One day, on Fifth Avenue, he and the girl fleetingly encounter, unspeaking. "He does not even recognize me," she thinks, "or he hates me now." And Witla debates whether to cut her as the act of vengeance she so richly deserves.

We may surmise that the elements of self-indulgence and self-vindication that appear so nakedly in *The "Genius"* constitute one of the reasons, perhaps the basic reason, for the book's being the crashing bore that it is. The kind of realism here practiced by Dreiser is based on the assumption that whatever is literally true (or whatever the born liar Dreiser takes to be true) is justified by that truth—that all that is required of the author is to report that truth. This assumption, in that it takes the literal truth as the basic criterion, justifies the telling of all, for no one thing, by this basis, is "truer" than anything else. Furthermore, the assumption makes superfluous the art in fiction, the shadings of emphasis, the imaginative renderings of depths and subtleties, the sense of the inwardness of action; the assumption reduces all to a monotone of mere chronicle with an occasional passage of commentary. Most destructively of all, the assumption makes into a virtue the self-indulgence and self-vindication of merely pouring out recollections, or pseudo-recollections. With this assumption, no self-criticism is possible, and no objective criticism of the work in progress.

Before publication, friends and editors of Dreiser drove themselves to the point of mania trying to sweat fat off the appalling bulk of the manuscript. After the work was published, Dreiser, with what his friend Mencken was wittily to describe as his "insatiable appetite for the obviously not true," maintained that, because the work had been so closely constructed, the editorial efforts expended on the manuscript had been able to reduce the original bulk by only three thousand five hundred words.

But delusion was to go one step further: Dreiser regarded The "Genius" as his finest novel.

In Sister Carrie and Jennie Gerhardt, though there

‡ 51 ‡

had been a deep personal involvement with the material, there was, by the mere fact that Dreiser was writing about women, if by nothing else, the necessity to keep distance; and this gave the imaginative scope to create the work and gave the critical faculty a chance to consider the work being created. But with the more complete identification of Dreiser with Witla, this was not possible. He did, however, make some feeble effort to achieve distance, as in Chapter XV, where he attempts to analyze the proneness of Witla to see in each new conquest "the sum and substance of bliss," and attempts to account for his behavior by the "chemistry of one's being," and to separate himself from his subject by saying that "Eugene did not know of those curious biologic experiments at this time. . . ." Again, in Chapter XXVIII, when Angela Blue (the name here given Sara White) is dying after the birth of her child, the treatment of Eugene's self-reproach and guilt is effective because it is set in the context of Eugene's wondering, "almost unconsciously," what kind of truth is in his remorse and his promises to do better.* Too often, however, the personal identification confuses the fictional effect and precludes the play of imagination that would make it possible for a reader to accept the reality of the characters; and paradoxically enough, the kind of personal realism here practiced by Dreiser destroys the fictional reality.

There is, however, another, more radical paradox involved in the deeper motivation of *The "Genius."* If, as I have suggested, the novel represents a kind of realism that would justify itself by mere factuality, the underlying drive—what Dreiser called the "metaphysical urge"—of the novel is toward the idea that the artist can achieve a "reality" beyond the criteria of the facts of experience. Eugene Witla the man is, by Dreiser's explicit statement, the victim of blind compulsions, or "chemisms," but in the end, after the shock of experience culminating in the loss of Flowerface, the death of Angela, and the birth of his daughter, he can achieve the "artistic normality of which he was capable—never again to be the maundering sentimentalist and enthusiast." He is now "tempered for life and work." In the concluding section, "L'Envoi," the discovery of the new locus of reality is given in a scene resembling a little allegory. One evening Eugene remembers and picks up to reread a passage from Herbert Spencer on the unknowableness of the universe. The passage ends with this sentence: "Of late years the consciousness that without origin or cause, infinite space has ever existed and must ever exist produces in me a feeling from which I shrink." Then Witla's little daughter enters to be cuddled before bedtime. Spencer and little Angela—those are the poles of life. But Witla turns from both to "great art dreams." There he finds the locus of his "reality"—beyond fact.

With *The "Genius,"* then, Dreiser writes his novel about the nature of art—or the novel—and about the role of the artist.* The book is about the birth of the artist—of Eugene, the "wellborn," as the name declares. It is another example, indeed, of the self-consciousness of the artist in the modern world that we find so often from Flaubert and Melville to Proust, Mann, Hemingway, Wolfe, and Camus; and the fact that Dreiser, the blundering autodidact who stood so far outside of literary culture, is the author gives this *bildungsroman* a peculiar historical interest. It is an unsuspected document toward the profile of an age.

A more immediate interest, however, attaches to *The "Genius."* Even in the novel most obviously tied to auto-biographical fact, Dreiser insists that fiction is an "art-dream." Fiction should achieve, ideally at least, as it does not achieve in this disastrous exemplar, the transformation of fact into form.

Dreiser may have been a most untrustworthy reporter, but he did have to a superlative degree the journalistic instinct for the hot topic, and that was what he had struck on in his three novels about the rise of a Robber Baron—*The Financier, The Titan,* and *The Stoic.* Already, *Sister Carrie* and *Jennie Gerhardt* had touched nerves that led deep into American life, and the period when Dreiser was beginning his career as a journalist and brooding ambivalently toward his massive work about business was the period when that subject was becoming more and more the storm center of public concern. The money panics of the age of the Robber Barons, their rapacity, the increasing violence of the labor wars, the growth of the great slums with their degradation and suffering, the fear of the middle class that, with the concentration of wealth on the one hand and the threat of socialism on the other, they would be liquidated—all these factors led to protest and reform, to Populism, William Jennings Bryan, Teddy Roosevelt, the Sherman Act. A part of this impulse was manifested in the work of the "muckrakers," which found its first great document in H. D. Lloyd's *Wealth Against Commonwealth*, in 1894.* This was, as we have said, the period when William Dean Howells, editor of the *Atlantic*, had caught the passion for social justice, and the period of the magazines of exposé, such as *The Forum*, the *Cosmopolitan*, *Muncey's* and *McClure's*. It was the period of the rise of Thorstein Veblen, Jacob Riis, Jack London, Ida Tarbell, Lincoln Steffens, Upton Sinclair, and Gustavus Myers, with his *History of the Great American Fortunes*. And as early as 1875 there had been a novel about a Robber Baron, Jim Fisk, in Josiah Gilbert Holland's *Sevenoaks*, and after that a series of novels dealing with the businessman, including *A Daughter of the Philistines*, by H. H. Boyesen (1883), *A Little Journey in the World*, by Charles Dudley Warner (1889), *A Hazard of New Fortunes*, by William Dean Howells (1889), *The Pit*, by Frank Norris (1903), and *Memoirs of an American Citizen*, by Robert Herrick (1905).

Whatever originality and significance lie in Dreiser's Trilogy do not derive from the fact that he saw business as a crucial concern of American life and as a threat to decency and democracy. That had already been demonstrated by a great body of writing. Dreiser's originality and significance lie in his ability to see under—and over—what reformers, politicians, muckrakers, and other novelists had seen, to relate the world of business to other elements and attitudes in American life and to the philosophy of an age, and to infuse the tale of American business with a deeply complex and self-contradictory personal emotion. The descriptive title "A Trilogy of Desire," which Dreiser early gave to his projected work, hints at the nature of what he dreamed.

Dreiser was concerned, in other words, to philosophize the Horatio Alger myth. In *Sister Carrie* he had, indeed, treated the myth, draining it of its moral content by setting it against the mechanics of success and failure; but now he undertook to anatomize it more fully, with all his deep ambivalences, in its psychological, social, moral, and metaphysical aspects. It scarcely seems an accident that the name "Alger" is absorbed into the name of his hero—Frank Algernon Cowperwood.

The Trilogy had its deep roots in the world that produced *Sister Carrie* and was more specifically conceived at the same time in Dreiser's life as *The "Genius"*; but it was projected as a fictional version of the life of Charles Tyson Yerkes, who, just after the Civil War, began his career as a manipulator of the street-car system of Philadelphia, made a fortune, crashed and went to prison, and then proceeded to a fantastic career in Chicago, New York, and London. He was, too, a collector of art and of women; and to arrange the legal and financial details for the dismissal, usually amicable, of mistresses or casual ladies of whom he had tired, he retained a staff of lawyers at the annual cost of one hundred and fifty thousand dollars. If the career of the fictional Eugene

Witla had been a projection of Dreiser's image of himself as artist, that of the real Yerkes gave an even grander scope for self-indulgent daydreams of identification with the Nietzschean superman. In fact, when in 1911 Dreiser explained to the British publisher Grant Richards his need to go to Europe to finish preparation for *The Financier*, he did not talk about getting a sense of the background of the European adventures of Yerkes, but of his desire to move in the same circles and to know the same kind of women who had caught his hero's fancy—in short, to relive literally the life of Yerkes. In the daydream thus projected, the cold logic of fact—the difference between his poverty and the fabulous wealth of Yerkes, between his stumbling uncouthness and the superman's worldly and hypnotic self-assurance—meant nothing. In fact, it is hard to believe that the superstitious Dreiser did not see as deeply significant certain parallels between Yerkes and himself more precise than the mere lust for power and social prestige, or the habits of the skirt-crazed "idealist," or a taste for art. For instance, both had known early success. Both had been ruined, and both had conquered despair, Yerkes in prison, Dreiser on the health farm. Both had made spectacular comebacks, Yerkes in Chicago, Dreiser with the *Delineator*, only to be again thwarted, both as a result of skirt-chasing (for the flagrant behavior of Yerkes contributed to the defeat of his grandiose plans in Chicago). Both were—at least as Dreiser saw it—"philosophers of power."

The superman that Dreiser saw in his hero—and in himself—was justified as a creature of nature, an exemplification of Darwinian theory: "Nature is unscrupulous! She takes her own way, regardless of the suffering caused, and the fittest survive." He longed, he said, to see a race "who like Niccolò Machiavelli could look life in the face," and saw his own role as that of an awakener who would make such a race possible. A literature of truth tied to the actual, the kind he claimed his own work to be, had been thwarted, he maintained, because society, specifically American society, had suppressed all attempts to expose the hypocrisy on which it was based. The men with a native power to produce a literature of truth tied to the actual were those who had become the great businessmen (still aware of the "poetry" and "romance" of their work); as a result of the "narrow-minded utilitarianism" of America, those very "men who might have given us an American art have followed the line of least resistance and gone into business." Interpreted, this would mean that Dreiser himself, who defied the "narrow-minded utilitarianism" by remaining an artist, was of the same tough breed as those who went into business—only more admirably tough for not taking the "line of least resistance." The theory was simply another way by which Dreiser defined himself as a superman.

If Dreiser was willing, by his identification with the new breed of businessmen beyond good and evil, to take the responsibility for their deeds, he would, at the same time, give those deeds a moral justification. On the whole, he affirmed, these predators "have been a blessing to the rest of us," and their services absolve them from blame. "It's because of Vanderbilt that we can now ride to Chicago in eighteen hours. It's because of Rockefeller that we get oil at the present price."* In general, "America is great not because of, but in spite of, her pieties and her moralities"—great, because businessmen, in spite of "her pieties and her moralities," could, as he put it in another connection, "do as they please," and "yet conform to all the prejudices of the community."

That is, the Robber Barons, having played lion, could take Machiavelli's advice and turn around and play fox and disinfect themselves by founding hospitals, libraries, universities, theological seminaries, and, like Yerkes, astronomical observatories. If Dreiser did have pity for the poor and deprived, he could still write that "most of us have a secret admiration for such business giants," and if he was capable, in his editorials in *Ev'ry Month*, of attacking those "men whose ambition carries them ruthlessly forward," he could, a little later, use *Lawless Wealth*, by Charles Edward Russell, one of the muckrakers, as merely a convenient source book for information about his hero Cowperwood.

This division of feeling is characteristic of the age in which Dreiser grew up; the age was, in fact, shot through with similar confusions and ambivalences. Even such famous muckrakers as Ida Tarbell and Lincoln Steffens had more than a sneaking admiration for the villains in the story, and Richard Hofstadter, in *The Progressive Historians*, writes of the divided mind of Charles A. Beard:

> On one side there was Beard the reformer, the moralist, the rebel against authority, the young Beard of Oxford, the Beard who all his days loved the gadfly's role. . . . On

the other side was the Beard of Knightstown [Beard's birthplace, in Indiana, where his father, from penniless beginnings, had made a small fortune], reared in solid Republicanism, himself strongly driven to achievement, a man who admired mastery and control . . . an American patriot who did indeed revere the practical genius of the Founding Fathers and who, in the light of all they accomplished, did not feel that the self-serving side of their work was an unforgivable flaw or that it should be taken to discredit their statecraft.*

As for Justice Holmes, who had read Herbert Spencer as a student at Harvard and not as a cub reporter in a newspaper office, and whose intellectual history is so central to an age, we have a similar split. On one hand, there is the Holmes who, at the age of twenty, while at the point of death from the first of his three wounds, could argue with himself:

> I am to take a leap in the dark—but now as ever I believe that whatever shall happen is best—for it is in accordance with a general law—and *good* and *universal* (or *general law*) are synonymous terms in the universe—(*I* can now add that our phrase *good* only means certain general truths seen through the heart and will instead of being merely contemplated intellectually—I doubt if the intellect accepts or recognizes that classification of good and bad).

This line of thought, that moral values have no objective justification, would lead him later to accept the grim social Darwinism expressed in a famous letter to Sir Frederick Pollock:

> I think that the sacredness of human life is a purely municipal ideal of no validity outside the jurisdiction. I believe that force, mitigated so far as may be by good manners, is the *ultima ratio*, and between two groups

that want to make inconsistent kinds of worlds I see no remedy except force. I may add what I no doubt have said often enough, that it seems to me that every society rests on the death of men. . . ."

And in 1895, when he received an honorary LL.D. from Harvard, he shocked that community by saying that in "this snug, over-safe corner of the world" war might be needed "that we may realize that our comfortable moment is no eternal necessity of things, but merely a little space of calm in the midst of the tempestuous untamed streaming of the world." This line of thought, too, found expression in Holmes' distaste for the Sherman Anti-Trust Act, which he regarded as unfair because it would not "let the strong man win the race."

But, on the other hand, there is the Holmes who earlier, in 1896, had been the author of the famous dissent of Vegelahn v. Guntner, which asserted, against the majority of the Supreme Court of Massachusetts, the legal right of strikers to picket—and which was later to make Teddy Roosevelt put Holmes on the United States Supreme Court, where, as the "Great Dissenter," he was to become the idol of the young liberals.*

If Holmes seems to be a divided man, Mark Twain literally was, and the tensions of his nature are never more clearly visible than with reference to the values of his time. On one hand, in disgust with the new finance capitalism, the Robber Barons, the corrupt politics, and the social shams, he could coin the phrase "The Gilded Age," and give it currency as the title of the novel he wrote with Charles Dudley Warner. He could, in "An Open Letter to Commodore Vanderbilt," write: "All I wish to urge you now, is that you crush out your native instincts and go and do something worthy of praise." He could curse the bitch-goddess Success and the philosophy of Grab, and for his dream of happiness look back to the Golden Age of Hannibal, Missouri, or the peace once found high in the pilot house of the texas deck of a steamboat—before the coming of the Civil War and the new order.

On the other hand, however, Mark Twain could be almost as abject before any stray millionaire as his hero poor old Grant, who could dream no higher destiny for his son than to be a businessman; and, in fact, Mark Twain's own dream was to become another Carnegie or Rockefeller. For years he had been bemused by one James W. Paige, the inventor of a typesetting machine, and it was by organizing a company to manufacture the invention that Mark Twain expected to join the company of the immortals. *A Connecticut Yankee in King Arthur's Court* embodied this dream. Literally, behind Hank Morgan, the Yankee, stands Paige; and, it should be added, Mark Twain himself, for if Hank (a superintendent in the Colt Arms Company) is an inventor (he claims he can "invent, contrive, create" anything), he quickly uses these talents to become the "Boss" in Arthur's England —that is, a titan of organization and business such as Mark Twain dreamed of becoming. There is, then, as much of an author's self-projection in Hank Morgan as in Frank Cowperwood.

A Connecticut Yankee in King Arthur's Court, which is the first novel to accept the heroic figure of the American businessman created by the popular imagination, stands, with *The Pit*, by Frank Norris, behind Dreiser's Trilogy, and more explicitly than the work of either Norris or Dreiser, indicates the nature of the revolt that the glorification of the businessman represented. Most immediately, the revolt was against the early novels of business in which the hero is crude or villainous, or both. The Yankee's image simply undercuts such attacks on the businessman, for the Yankee embodies the very traits that had been previously presented as disreputable: he worships efficiency, his values are strictly practical, he has no mustard seed of sentiment, poetry, or reverence (at least not until he has been chastened by experience), he loves projects and gadgetry, his discourse is larded with metaphors drawn from the world of business enterprise, he is not concerned in the slightest with taste and refinement.

Beyond the immediate revolt against earlier fictional portraits of the businessman, *The Connecticut Yankee* represents a revolt against the sentimental medievalism of the period. The Romantic Movement had discovered— or created—the Middle Ages, and had prepared for them their sacred place in nineteenth-century thought and art. Tennyson's *Idylls of the King* ranked in the esteem of the pious only a little lower than the New Testament, and James Russell Lowell's "The Vision of Sir Launfal" was a close contender for the popularity prize with the Book of Common Prayer. The poetry of William Morris and the paintings of the Pre-Raphaelites, with Ruskin's Gothic aestheticism and the related social theories that pitted medieval spirituality and happy craftsmanship against the age of the machine and restless democracy, had great vogue in the United States, a vogue that found its most delicate bloom in Charles Eliot Norton, who wistfully pointed out to his students at Harvard that there were in America no French cathedrals, and in Henry Adams, with his *Mont St. Michel and Chartres*, and his remark that the only thing he "wanted in life was to be made a cardinal."

This cult of medievalism had a strongly marked class element. Usually it attracted persons of aristocratic background or aspiration, often with an overlay of Catholicism. It was also associated with wealth, but with inherited wealth as contrasted with the wealth, usually much greater, of the new breed of capitalists; for inherited wealth, untainted by any immediate contact with the crude world of business, was "genteel." It was only natural, then, that a poem like Sidney Lanier's "The Symphony" and the earlier novels treating business should use the aristocratic virtues as the thongs with which to scourge the businessman. So, when Hank, with his six-shooters, guns down Malory's knights in armor, he is also gunning down Tennyson, Lowell, Lanier, *et al.* —and, incidentally, all thin-skinned moralists and muck-rakers who would deny the logic of the new order, and all the exponents of the "genteel tradition." He was, even, gunning down General Robert E. Lee, C.S.A.

Mark Twain's novel does not, however, end with Hank's great victory. Even if Mark Twain had set out to brush away the cobwebs of medieval irrationality and exhibit a society run on the business model, with the Round Table turned into a stock board, his ambivalence reasserted itself. Things do not work out according to the Yankee's scheme. The dream of the regeneration of society by technology (or by a fast trip to Chicago and a lower price on oil) ends in a blood bath made more hideous by the manic glee of the technicians exalted by their expertise of destruction as they stand in a crimson drizzle of minute bits of horse-flesh and man-flesh just now hurled into the sky by clever land mines. Hank comes to regard the people he would have liberated as nothing more than "human muck." He hates all life, and all he can do is to look nostalgically back on the beauty of premodern Britain, on what he calls his "Lost World," and on the love of his lost wife Sandy, who had belonged to that simple past; just as Mark Twain could look back on his vision of boyhood Hannibal, and as Dreiser could look back on Sarah Dreiser, Jennie Gerhardt, Roberta, and Mrs. Griffiths as people who could live outside the world of success and power.

Mark Twain, as a novelist, is closer to Dreiser* than is Beard or Holmes, but the historian and the jurist were as deeply concerned with the impact of the great impersonal forces of technology and society on the personal fate of men. If it be objected that Dreiser, with his "chemisms," grounds his drama on nature rather than—or as well as—on technology and society, it may be replied that for Dreiser society is conceived as an extension of nature; and this would ultimately be as true of Holmes. Holmes—along with William Graham Sumner and many other intellectuals of the age—would have understood perfectly the meaning of the parabolic moment in *The Financier* when the boy Frank Cowperwood stares into the tank where a lobster and squid are exhibited and where, at last, the lobster eats the squid. Young Frank ponders the event:

> Things lived by each other—that was it. Lobsters lived on squid and other things. What lived on lobsters? Men, of course! Sure, that was it! And what lived on men?

Frank finds the answer: "Sure, men lived on men." So society, as Holmes puts it in the letter to Pollock, "rests on the deaths of men."

This is the premise of Cowperwood's career, even in *The Stoic*, one chapter of which Dreiser, as an old man full of religiosity and a member of the Communist Party, rewrote on December 27, 1945, only the day before his death. The boy Frank Cowperwood, having learned his main lesson by staring into the fishmonger's tank, and an important corollary in the local brothels and bagnios, is ready for life, and the first novel of the "Trilogy of Desire" is a record of his precocious conquest of the streetcar system of Philadelphia up to the time when, in 1871, as a backlash of the Chicago Fire, his speculations with public funds are revealed and he serves a short sentence in the penitentiary (as did Dreiser's model Yerkes). "He was not," Dreiser says of Cowperwood in the early stages of his career, "a man who was inherently troubled with conscientious scruples. At the same time he still believed himself financially honest." But a little later this analysis is modified and elaborated: ". . . by this time his financial morality had become special and local in its character. He did not think it was wise for anyone to steal anything from anybody where the act of taking or profiting was directly and plainly considered stealing. . . . Morality varied, in his mind at least, with conditions, and climates." The word "right" for Cowperwood, as for Holmes in his role not of man but of philosopher, might be considered a matter of "municipal jurisdiction," and the municipality in which Cowperwood operated was the politically corrupt Philadelphia of the Gilded Age. If he happens to wind up in the penitentiary, that is little more than an industrial accident.

Cowperwood's spirit is no more broken than shamed by the accident. If anything, it is annealed, and confirmed in both its sense of high destiny and the philosophy that was becoming more explicit as he inspected the logic of experience, a philosophy to be summed up by the motto "I satisfy myself." Pardoned, he leaves the penitentiary, steeled for new struggles; and when, on September 13, 1873, the great Philadelphia firm of Jay Cooke & Company fails and the panic is on, Cowperwood knows that this is his moment, and with lethal certainty proceeds to batten on the general ruin. He is now ready, at the end of the first novel, to move to Chicago, where the sky is the limit.

Along with the financial education of the hero has gone his *éducation sentimentale*. After the women of the brothels and bagnios (where he finds the décor tasteless) have begun to pall, the young Cowperwood develops a passion for the widow of a middle-aged friend—a woman five years his senior, but fresh and young-looking, tall and shapely, of pale waxen complexion, gray-blue eyes, and a face "artistically narrow," and with a calm, sometimes brooding dignity, a dignity that

Cowperwood later discovers to spring from stupidity. With Lillian Semple it was, first, her seeming dignity, or even indifference, that fired his instinct. That "pale, uncertain, lymphatic body extracted a form of dynamic energy from him," and stirred a need to make her "love him vigorously" and to "rout out the memory of her former life"—that is, to "kill" the middle-aged friend who had been the husband, and thus become a man. The fact that Lillian had been married is, then, one of her attractions, an added challenge. "Strange perversion," comments Dreiser after he had stated the need of young Cowperwood to "rout out" her memories of Semple.*

Cowperwood gets that pale, uncertain, lymphatic body that had so challenged him, and fleetingly at least, he does stir it and wakens it to a new sense of the depth of life and sexuality. He builds Lillian a new house, has a son in whom he takes pleasure (the "idea of self-duplication" being also "acquisitive"), and for a short time preens himself on having the woman whom, six years before, when he was nineteen and she was presiding over the home of Mr. Semple, he had regarded as the ideal wife. And she would have been the ideal wife for a rising young businessman—devoted, prudent, careful of public opinion, beautiful, dignified, a competent if not an experienced hostess.

But Cowperwood is not merely another rising young businessman, and she is stupid. His ideas, his growing interest in art, his ambitions are far beyond her imagination. The long, creamy body no longer stirs him, for he knows all that it is capable of. There is no longer a challenge. And to cap matters, after five years she turns sickly.

Then Aileen Butler appears. She is only a girl, the daughter of the restricted Catholic household of a crude Irish contractor, but Cowperwood sees in her the capacity for passion, the strength of will, the contempt for convention, and the sensibility and intelligence to match his own. As Lillian had offered, in her sluggishness, one type of sexual challenge, which Cowperwood has now explored, so Aileen offers its opposite, not a recessive passion to be provoked, but an aggressive one to be matched and mastered. She becomes his mistress (in a process presented in a series of powerful scenes), and even in his apparent ruin, she retains, unlike his wife, her faith in his great destiny. When he leaves for Chicago at the end of the novel, it is with the understanding that she will join him there, to become his wife as soon as he is free.

The Financier would seem, then, to have, in its own way, a happy ending. The superman has found the appropriate mate to share his labors and conquests. The labors are indeed performed, and the conquests made— at least Cowperwood acquires a great fortune, becomes a national figure, and moves on to New York, where he builds a splendid mansion crammed with his collection of art. But in Chicago he has left his name synonymous with political corruption, and in New York, no more than in Chicago, can he breach the inner defenses of society. At the end, he is still the outsider, the marauder, now preparing to attack the citadel of Europe.

Aileen is, however, no longer significant in his life. A dozen women, all kinds, have passed through his hands, each representing some need of his ego, each captured by the hard, assertive, unrelenting sufficiency of his "glazed" blue stare. Aileen is still married to him and still, even in her outrage, in love with him; but when, by chance, she sees him with the latest of his loves, a young girl at whom he looks with "soul-hunger," that look drives her to a protracted orgy with a man for whom she cares nothing. Later, when Cowperwood declares that the "thing I used to feel I cannot feel any more," she attempts suicide. Even then Cowperwood remains unmoved. He is a gambler, and now he gambles that she will not again try suicide, and so goes his way: "If her intention was genuine, she would carry it out in his absence, but he did not believe she would."

Now, in a moment of political reverse, the girl at whom he had stared with "soul-hunger," but on whom he had not yet laid a finger, comes to him. She is, he feels, the woman who will sum up life for him, who is the "ultimate end of fame, power, vigor."

She steps into his arms:

"Berenice!" he smothered her cheeks and hair.
"Not so close, please. And there aren't to be any other ladies, unless you want me to change my mind."
"Not another one, as I hope to keep you. You will share everything I have . . ."
For answer—
How strange are realities as opposed to illusion!

So this novel, like the previous one, might be said to have, at least with the love story, a happy ending—one eminently fit, except for the small matter of a legal ceremony, for the Butterick publications.

There is, however, a brief epilogue in which appears the following passage:

> Anew the old urgent thirst for life, and only its partial quenchment. In Dresden, a palace for one woman, in Rome a second for another. In London a third for his beloved Berenice, the lure of beauty ever in his eye. The lives of two women wrecked, a score of victims despoiled; Berenice herself weary, yet brilliant, turning to others for recompense for her lost youth.

In one sense, "In Retrospect," as the epilogue to *The Titan* is called, renders *The Stoic* superfluous. It may have been intended to serve merely as a stopgap, a provisional end—and indeed, it had to serve as such for some thirty years—but it may still strike a reader as a technically shocking and, at the same time, brilliantly satisfying conclusion to the story. Coming after the scene with Berenice, and Cowperwood's belief that she crowns his life, this reversal, better than any subsequent documentation in *The Stoic*, underscores the tragic fact that the victor is finally the victim of illusion. Here, however, we are ahead of ourselves, for *The Stoic* does exist and, for better or worse, must be reckoned with.

For the remaining years of Cowperwood's life, *The Stoic* adds little beyond documentation, now drearily repetitious, of his financial operations in London and of the love affairs forecast in the epilogue of *The Titan*. But with the hero's death, on the verge of success in his last great foray, more interest is developed. The bitter Aileen tries to prevent the body from being laid out in state in the midst of the grandeur Cowperwood had assembled in the mansion. The fortune is picked to pieces in litigations, as though by jackals—in a technical balance of the fact that, long ago in Philadelphia, it had been founded on the ruin of Jay Cooke. Cowperwood's project of an art museum, undertaken from whatever mixture of motives, goes unfulfilled, and his collection is scattered under the auctioneer's hammer, snatched up by other jackals. And the last movement of the novel concerns the strange fate of Berenice, who experiences a conversion to Eastern mysticism, ponders the wisdom of her guru, sells the house her lover had given her, and devotes herself to good works and the hope of realizing another dream of Cowperwood, that of founding a charity hospital.

Dreiser's Trilogy constitutes a very puzzling fiction, and to turn autobiographical, I may say that, over the years, my own shifting reactions to it have been a constant source of puzzlement to me. At times, I have regarded each of the novels as a total failure and a bore, crudely written and dramatically unrealized—and to give point to this, I should say that since I first read *An American Tragedy*, shortly after its publication, my admiration for it has never flagged. But no matter at how low a rate I have regarded the Trilogy, it has stuck in my mind, and sometimes on coming back to it—at least, on coming back to the first two novels—I have been surprised to find myself plunging on, completely bemused. As John Berryman has said of his numerous rereadings of *The "Genius"* (which is consistently a bore for me), my own rereadings of *The Financier* and *The Titan* have often been done with a "febrile, self-indulgent eagerness." Even with such eagerness, Berryman denies that he has ever felt for *The "Genius"* "admiration, precisely," but I confess that if what I have on occasion felt for *The Financier* and *The Titan* is not admiration, it is something more rare, and perhaps more valuable: commitment.

The fact of commitment, even if a flickering commitment, has led me to speculate that my sometime judgment of those two novels as failures might have its roots in my having applied irrelevant criteria to them, in my having brought to them, more or less unconsciously, a conception of fiction quite at variance with what Dreiser had in mind. This is not necessarily to say that I might not have been right in my conception, but it is to explain my wish here to understand, if possible, the kind of fiction represented by the "Trilogy of Desire."

The Trilogy was massively researched. This devoted effort was, as I have already suggested, inspired, in part at least, by Dreiser's daydreaming identification with Yerkes, and such identification no doubt gave the initial emotional energy for the effort, and carries over into the work itself. But the research indicates, too, a significant aspect of the fiction. Cowperwood is not a fictional creation based on Yerkes; he is, insofar as Dreiser could make him, the image of Yerkes. And this fact of fidelity to historical fact sets the Trilogy off, paradoxically, from the ordinary historical novel; for the historicity of the ordinary historical novel lies in situation and décor into which the actors, with their "perennial humanity," are introduced.* But Cowperwood, the Yerkes-image, is not introduced into historical situation and décor merely to act out his "perennial humanity"; he is there because he himself *is* the history, he is his own validation.

Here we may ask why Dreiser, after considering other models, chose Yerkes and not Vanderbilt, Frick, Fisk, Brady, Carnegie or Rockefeller—one of the names that were equally available and now bulk so much larger in our consciousness. But our consciousness is not Dreiser's—nor that of the general public at the time when he was meditating his work; for the dramatic quality of Yerkes' manipulations gave them something of the popular interest of a great sporting event, and even after his death, the series of litigations continued to provoke such an interest. Furthermore, the death of Yerkes came at a dramatic moment in his career, and the fact of the death underscored the life. Even in far-off Ottumwa, Iowa, as F. O. Matthiessen has pointed out, headlines announced the moral of the tale: *Death the Great Leveller.* The death of Yerkes, like the sinking of the *Titanic,* was an event that, in its massive and simple irony, came ready-made for the folk-consciousness. And Dreiser's consciousness was firmly rooted in the folk-consciousness.**

But most importantly of all, Yerkes gave Dreiser the combination of factors he needed for his projected work: the strongly individualized man fulfilling himself in the realms of finance, love, and art. And this collocation was fundamental for Dreiser's conception; it constitutes, as we shall later see, another kind of trilogy of desire. And ten years before Dreiser began work on *The Financier,* he had clipped a newspaper account of Yerkes' career that was clearly written by a man with the instincts of a literary critic:

> We couldn't expect Mr. Howells to deal with such a story. . . . We shudder to think what might happen if Mr. James undertook it. . . . By divine right it is the property of Balzac, with Daudet as residuary legatee. Both are dead.

But Theodore Dreiser was not.

For the moment it is of more concern, however, to ask what purpose a Yerkes, once found, would serve— would serve, that is, beyond satisfying Dreiser's constant need in his fiction for both self-indulgence and self-scrutiny. Certainly at that late date, after Lloyd, Myers, Ida Tarbell, *et al.,* to delineate the machinations of a financier, or after all the thunder from pulpits and the exposés in the magazines, to be virtuously appalled by sexual license in high places, would scarcely seem a compellingly original enterprise. No, Dreiser was undertaking to reveal a more dire secret than the muckraker had ever suspected; he was undertaking to give the truly "inside story" of the "financier," to show the workings of his mind and soul, to show how his acquisitiveness, sex, and "art-dreams" flowed into one another, to place him not only in society but in nature, in the economy of the universe. If Dreiser was to be a muck-raker, he was to be a cosmic muckraker. To achieve this end he needed to analyze the most perfectly formed specimen of "financier" available.

The word "specimen" is here the key to what Dreiser was trying to do, to the kind of novel he was trying to write. Carrie and Jennie had not been specimens. They had come to Dreiser as individuals, in the deep texture of their, and his own, personal life. The act of imagination in telling their stories had been inductive: to affirm their individuality in such a way that the generalization of meaning would be merely a function of their existence. To create a Cowperwood, imagination was also necessary, but Cowperwood came into being only as the image of Yerkes, and imagination was involved only insofar as it involved the inwardness of the specimen already chosen: only insofar as it might illustrate the inwardness implied by the outwardness of the specimen.

Yerkes exemplifies the class "financier," the class "titan." Dreiser, to all intents and purposes, is saying: "I am telling you about Frank Algernon Cowperwood, but you must remember that I am doing so in order for you to understand the nature of such a man and his meaning in society and nature." The method is narrative, but the motive is expository. And this returns us to the difference between the historical novel and the kind of fiction represented here. Here Dreiser is trying to invent a genre, a novel in which all the outer facts are certified and the inner facts are imaginatively extrapolated from that evidence, and the whole, outer and inner, is offered as a document.

Perhaps it is too strong to say that Dreiser was trying to invent a genre. He was, rather, working in terms of an impulse that had already been clearly, but sometimes paradoxically, defined. On one hand, it could be argued that the spirit of America, in accordance with its practical bias and pragmatic philosophy, had no need of the arts, but could fulfill itself in the world of business. On the other hand, it could be argued, as by Dreiser himself in the Trilogy and earlier, that business was itself an art. But another position was also possible: the form of art might be retained but the content might be shifted from the imaginative to the factual. This attitude, of course, was related to the realistic fiction that had risen after the Civil War, but it could be carried far beyond such a manifestation. For instance, Henry B. Fuller, the author of the historically important novels of the 1890's, *The Cliff-Dwellers* and *With the Procession,** on whom Dreiser, in *The Titan*, was to heavily depend for his picture of Chicago society, most clearly enunciated this hybrid view, when he insisted that in the new America fiction should be replaced by biography. This was simply a narrow formulation of what was actually happening, with the rise of "human interest" reporting (in which Dreiser got his journalistic start) and of the muckraking article and novel—that is, the material of fact rendered with the airs and graces of fiction. And the Trilogy may be taken as Dreiser's version of this hybrid form.

The fact that this whole is regarded as a document has certain significant effects on its form as a novel. For one thing, take the matter of time. Time in the ordinary novel is the very medium of existence; the *dressage* of time, the control of its densities, lapses, and involutions is the essence of the art; in the sense suggested by Thomas Mann in *The Magic Mountain*, the novel may be, not a tale *in* time, but a tale *of* time; and the tensions between temporal form (the kinetic flow) and spatial form (the kinetic flow conceived as an objectified stasis) is the central factor on which the overall structure of the novel depends. But in the documentary novel time has no such importance. The narration here is essentially a chronicle. In only the crudest sense is time here a medium for Dreiser. Time is, rather, conceived as a bin into which he reaches for items relevant to his exposition. The flatness of narration, the monotony of the construction of scenes—such things result from the fact that Dreiser is not really concerned with process in time, with the vibration of life in time, with gradation and distinction, but with illustration. Cowperwood does not grow old, as does Pierre Bezuhov in *War and Peace*, or Constance in *The Old Wives' Tale*, or Swann or Marcel in *A la recherche du temps perdu*, or Jennie in her novel. Time is not the medium of the documentary novel. Dialectic is the medium.*

The fact of dialectic as the medium has, too, certain effects on the conception of character in such fiction. Clarity and strength of outline become prime virtues, not complexity and shading. This, furthermore, is to be regarded in two perspectives. First, in the perspective of the meaning of character in the paradigmatic sense— its summary significance in the dialectic. Second, in the perspective of self-definition—the essential drama of the character's discovery of his own nature and role.

From the second perspective stems whatever redeeming grandeur Cowperwood possesses (though some critics would deny him any degree of this). The grandeur comes from the fact that the predator presented by Dreiser is not merely an automaton of nature. He is the predator-as-philosopher who analyzes his own role and who speculates concerning his own place in the universe. This unillusioned awareness, which is rooted in the moment when the young Frank stares into the tank at the fishmonger's, is what gives the man his stature—whatever he has of tragic scale. Like Richard III, he is "determined" to be a villain, and like the hunchback king he accepts his definition with a kind of irony, gay or grim according to the occasion.* Cowperwood, again like Richard, exhibits a pure relish in the game of life, in the parade of his own virtuosity; and Dreiser, like the creator of Richard, dramatically emphasizes the scale of his hero, and at the same time puts him beyond the reach of immediate moral criticism, by setting him in a world populated by men driven by the same impulse but with neither the skill nor nerve to gratify them so fully, nor the courage to explore and face their own natures. The importance of this fact in our acceptance of Cowperwood comes clear if we remember that he is never allowed to confront a "good" man—or woman. What a different effect if Cowperwood and Jennie should meet!

The predator-as-philosopher, furthermore, achieves grandeur in yet another dimension. This is best illustrated by the scene (reminiscent of Hardy) in *The Financier* where Cowperwood, in the penitentiary, his career apparently blasted, stares up at the stars:

. . . he thought of the earth floating like a little ball in the immeasurable reaches of ether. His own life appeared very trivial in view of these things, and he found himself asking whether it was all really of any significance or importance. He shook these moods off with ease, however, for the man was possessed of a sense of grandeur, largely in relation to himself and his affairs. . . .

As a kind of gloss on this passage, we may take Cowperwood's attitude when, for the first time after beginning his sentence, wearing his prison clothes, he must confront Aileen: "Only a stoic sense of his own soul-dignity aided him here." He is, in other words, himself, no matter where he is, or what he wears. In part, of course, this comes from his certainty of superior endowments and his will to persist, but more, as we shall see when the two passages are juxtaposed, is involved. To be himself, in the face of personal disaster *and* in the face of the indifferent constellations: in both the practical and the metaphysical sense, a man must create his values ("I satisfy myself," says Cowperwood), and the creation of values is the creation of the self, the assertion of "soul-dignity." Such values may be in contrast with those of society; but more fundamentally, they are inevitably in contrast with the blankness of the universe.

The hero who is instructed in the nature of things and can face his knowledge, knows that values have sanction and validity only in the passion of their assertion. He is aware of the root-irony that even he, the man of will, is part of the machine of the universe, and is, like the veriest weakling, a creature of "chemisms."

By the same token by which determinism may be used as extenuation—as when Cowperwood tells Aileen that it is not his fault that he cannot feel what once he felt, that "love is not a bunch of coals that can be blown by an artificial bellows into flame"—the hero knows that even the act of will, and therefore the sense of "soul-dignity," is, ultimately, an illusion.

Illusion—it is the key word for Dreiser.* And on this basis we may see the deeper relationship he would find in his predator's self-assertion on one hand, and love and art on the other. It is true, as Matthiessen and other critics have pointed out, that a woman may be nothing more than a convenience or a status symbol for the "financier," and that the Robber Barons characteristically collected art, not for art's sake, but as a mark of culture, privilege, and prestige, and for investment. Dreiser gives full weight to such realistic motives, for example, in the young Cowperwood's attitude toward Lillian Semple, whom he marries for a social convenience as well as to gratify the lust he feels for that creamy, lymphatic body, or in the scene when his dealer first suggests that art is a good investment. But behind such motives of self-aggrandizement, convenience, and profit, taken at a realistic level, Dreiser would expose a more metaphysical truth. As the "financier," yearning for meaning in the meaningless universe of indifferent stars, finds it in the illusion of will, so he seeks meaning in the other primary illusions, love and art.

As for love, the significance of will as a factor should not be underrated, but it is only one factor. This is the significance of the fact that in his story there is a progression from blank sex with the women of the brothels and bagnios (with their tasteless décor) to the focused lust and aesthetic appreciation in the episode of Lillian Semple, to the actress Stephanie, who saw him "as a very great artist in his realm," on to Berenice, who understood that "spirit of art that accompanied the center" of his "iron personality," and who, for a time anyway, came to stand for the love "which the strongest almost more than the weakest crave." We should recall, too, that one of the intolerable limitations of Lillian is her inability to understand her husband's "art-dreams." Cowperwood can stare at the beautiful woman or the beautiful picture with "soul-hunger," for both, in their beauty, seem annunciations of meaning. But both, like the act of will, are illusions. We remember that when, at the end of The "Genius," Witla turns to his "great art-dreams," those dreams, like the love of little Angela (or of big Angela and other women), are set against the blank vision of infinite space described by Herbert Spencer in the volume that Witla has just taken down from the shelf.

Two episodes in *The Titan* are especially instructive on this point, and at the same time indicate the thematic density of the Trilogy. The first episode is Cowperwood's love affair with Stephanie.* This is the only affair in which the predator fails to work his will. Stephanie, as he early realizes, is "too much like him"—that is, she too knows that love is not a matter of ultimate sanctions, is an illusion. Furthermore, she is an artist, and as such she is not even capable of the provisional commitment to passion of which Cowperwood is capable:

"She was an unstable chemical compound, artistic to her fingertips." The aesthetic commitment of the actress —that significantly is what she is—is to the role and the scene, nothing more, and each role, each scene, is its own validation. She, the "free-lover," plays various roles of love, and here the illusion of art undercuts, we may put it, even the illusion of love: illusion within illusion. The "strange fatalism" about Stephanie that had so touched Cowperwood is, we may take it, some shadowy awareness that all is illusion. To put it differently, her sense of the illusory in both love and art had undercut the illusion of will; her sense of will is deficient, therefore we have the "strange fatalism." In the end it is this illusion within illusion that Cowperwood, the man of will, cannot prevail against.*

The second episode in question is the scene of Cowperwood's declaration of love to Berenice. Matthiessen says that we have here a "weakly supported turn of character, in no way foreshadowed." But there is a foreshadowing, thematic and structural. To begin with, only twice in the long catalog of Cowperwood's amours does the predator find the tables turned on him. Once, as we have first seen, is with Stephanie, at about the mathematical center of *The Titan,* the second with Berenice at the end; and both times by "artists." Cowperwood has come to the interview with Berenice "primarily to magnetize and control" her will, but finds that she is "almost dominating" him, "making him explain himself," changing him from the cold predator into the pleading lover who can affirm that there is "such a thing as an ideal," and that his happiness will lie in her happiness.

even if that means renouncing her. This is not mere tactics, for Cowperwood believes what he says; but the irony is double-edged, for the belief is only, as events will demonstrate, "for the time being," and so we have the irony of the deceiver self-deceived. Or to put it differently, the irony is that sincerity is an illusion. For the second irony, this discovery of the "ideal" love that can be loved "ideally," is, after all, "foreshadowed," for the entrance of Stephanie into the novel is announced by the statement, in the paragraph before her name is first mentioned, that "it might have been said of him [Cowperwood] that he was seeking the realization of an ideal"—the ideal that later he thinks is realized in Berenice. So here, as that second irony, we find, at the end of the novel, that the philosopher of "illusion" discovers the need of "truth."

Cowperwood, the philosopher of illusion, goes on to recover his philosophy; his old chemisms and his old skepticisms get back to work, the old pattern of behavior reasserts itself, and Cowperwood is "resigned and yet not" to the fate of the man who, "drawn by chemisms," can, nevertheless, truly live only by illusion. For life is only the "expression of contraries," as Dreiser puts it in *A Traveler at Forty*. If man is, on one side, the creature of blind desire, there is, on the other, the "saving element of love," as Dreiser says of the young Aileen, with her "passionate illusion." If the wall of the world is blank, yet man can project upon it a vision of "amethyst and gold," and it does not matter that this projection is the product of "some mulch of chemistry" in the make-up of the visionary. If even the self is created by the illusory act of will, it may, as the blazing trajectory of Cowperwood is described at the end of *The Titan,* briefly "illuminate the terror and wonder of individuality."*

The ultimate wisdom, Dreiser would seem to say, is to be unillusioned, but to know, in a strange paradoxical doubleness, the necessity of illusion: "Woe be to him who places his faith in illusion—the only reality—and woe to him who does not." For only by the acceptance of the illusion that creates individuality, can it be said, to quote the last words of *The Titan,* "Thou hast lived."

As a corollary to the ultimate wisdom, there is the ultimate virtue, to understand the pathos of those who are born to struggle in the world where illusion is the only reality, as Cowperwood fleetingly understands it when, holding his first son in his arms, he becomes aware of the "old conviction of tragedy under the surface of things," or at the time when Cowperwood, musing on the Aileen who has at last sought refuge and vengeance in adultery, can look back on the beginning of her "passionate illusion" and think of her as the "sweet fool of love." But the pity that the unillusioned superman can offer the victims of illusion is of the same order, though smaller in scale and tenderer in texture, as the pity provoked in Dreiser as corollary to the "terror and wonder" evoked by the brief transit of the superman himself; for the superman represents what the philosopher Josiah Royce, as he put it in *Modern Idealism,* saw in Nietzsche: ". . . an idealism without any ideal world of truth, a religion without any faith, a martyrdom without prospect of a paradise. . . ."; and even if in Dreiser's universe, the superman does find the "ideal world of truth" in illusion, of "faith" in illusion, and of "paradise" in illusion, this merely accents the ultimate demand for pity.

So part of the wisdom of the unillusioned man is to recognize that even more redemptive than illusion is the pity for illusion; and, at this point, we see how, for Dreiser, naturalistic insight is akin to Christian charity—as Santayana remarks in his essay on Dickens—or how, as David Brion Davis puts it in an essay called "Dreiser and Naturalism Revisited," Dreiser knew "the emotion of a pietist, whose aesthetic and moral love of Being transcends any ethical protest or social rebellion."

What I have been trying to do is to indicate something of the thematic density of the Trilogy, something of the dialectic that charges the work. I recognize that all fiction in some degree, insofar as it embodies values (and what fiction, however stupidly or limpingly, does not?), exhibits a dialectical progression. But here, as I have suggested earlier, the degree is crucial, amounting to a difference in kind, amounting here to what may be called the documentary novel. This would imply that the emphasis on dialectic tends to use the substance as document, to shift the interest from its "being" to its "signifying." I am not saying that because of this emphasis—because of the genre of this novel—the realization of "being," verbally or dramatically in scene, character, and action, is not crucial: fiction is not philosophy. What I am saying is that the power of the dialectic significantly compensates for certain bleaknesses in realization. No fiction can, indeed, provide total realization—and if it could do so, it would, paradoxically, fail as fiction, for the power of fiction lies in the involvement of the reader's imagination to fulfill the "un-total" realization, to participate in the act of creation. The stimulus of the imagination is, however, different from instance to instance, for our passions and curiosities are various, and what keeps the reader going in, say, *The Golden Bowl* would not be the same passions and curiosities that keep him going in *Moby Dick*. And Dreiser's Trilogy is much nearer *Moby Dick* than it is to *The Golden Bowl;* for instance, Cowperwood, who can scarcely be said to belong to the same race as Prince Amerigo, is blood brother to Ahab, that idealist who, like Cowperwood, had no "ideal world of truth." If we are drawn to Cowperwood (as to Ahab) by the same taint in ourselves of Dreiser's massive and passionate daydream of power, and if we are also held by mechanical curiosity about the techniques and processes of finance (as of whale fishery), we are even more compelled by the dialectical deployments in character and action. Intellectual passion and curiosity are powerful in us, too, and we, like poor Cowperwood, yearn for meaning, and foretell his fate, literally as well as virtually. Furthermore, we must remember that as we yearn for meaning, we necessarily yearn for fulfillment in form in a work, for form involves the fulfillment of dialectic as deeply as it involves anything else: form is meaning.

Even if it be granted—as it must be granted—that nothing counts if a work of fiction sinks below a certain threshold of realization, we must remember that such a threshold is never determined extraneously, abstractly, or ideally. All we can ever ask is that the current of life, the sense of action as form, manifest itself, and there the only ultimate argument is simple testimony. To turn autobiographical again, I find the scenes in the courtship of Aileen psychologically precise and compelling, and her whole character strongly created. Even Lillian exists, objectively at least, visually at least, and something comes through of the strangely passive and blankly pensive provocativeness of her pale presence that fed the young Cowperwood's obsession. Though the Stephanie sequence is abominably written, there are splendid strokes and insights: for instance, that concerning her "fatalism" and its mysterious effect on her lover, or the special quality of her sexuality suggested by the characteristic moment when Cowperwood, breaking into her withdrawn mood, would touch her and she would turn toward him, suddenly saying, "Oh yes, oh, yes." The last view of Stephanie is memorable, and psychologically right: Cowperwood has burst in on her and the young poet, and as she huddles on the divan, her nakedness only partly concealed, her wide, dark eyes stare theatrically at him in piteous reproach. To the last, she is playing a role.

The Financier was published in October 1912 to a good, if not wildly enthusiastic, press and to Mencken's dictum, "a magnificent piece of work." If Dreiser was still poor (he had been living on advances from Harper's), he was at least making a reputation as a novelist to be reckoned with, and when, at the end of the year, he went to Chicago to do research on Yerkes for *The Titan*, he found himself something of a lion to the literary and artistic world there, which included Sherwood Anderson, Edgar Lee Masters, Arthur Davidson Ficke, John Cowper Powys, Margaret Anderson, and Kirah Markham, the young actress whom we have already mentioned in a note.

Work on *The Titan* was slow, and then, when it was finally in sheets and had been advertised, Harper's suddenly decided not to publish it, afraid either of what Dreiser called the "woman stuff" (which had already been drastically reduced by editorial pressure) or of a suit by one Emilie Grigsby, the Berenice of the novel. After rejections by a galaxy of publishers, the book was brought out in 1914 by the American branch of the John Lane Company of London. Mencken remained a faithful admirer, but reviews were generally short of enthusiastic and the sale was substantially lower than that of *The Financier*. Dreiser's mood was not helped much the next year when *The "Genius,"* which no publisher had wanted, was at last issued by Lane to a bad press, even Mencken calling it an "endless emission of the obvious," and saying that it suggested the "advanced thinking of Greenwich Village."

An American Tragedy, Dreiser's next novel, was not to appear for ten years. That period was full of distractions, confusions, blind alleys, and despairs, but one great distraction of the period did give definition to

Dreiser's role on the literary scene. When in 1916 John S. Sumner, of the New York Society for the Suppression of Vice, succeeded in banning The "Genius," Dreiser's position as a revolutionary hero was confirmed, and the public gestures in his defense by the Authors' League and other persons and groups, and the subsequent litigation, were of considerable value as advertising.*

The whole affair, whatever its value, was time-consuming and confusing. Even more confusing was the immersion Dreiser was now experiencing in the ferment of new ideas characteristic of the time. He took up with political radicalism, and knew Emma Goldman; with psychoanalysis and knew Dr. Abraham Brill, the local apostle of the cult, and suffered severe depression from reading the doctor's expositions. He consorted with intellectuals of various stripes, who often regarded him as a child; even if some did recognize his force, they, being accustomed to treat ideas as counters in their characteristic game, could not understand the man who automatically absorbed ideas into the bloodstream of his passionate being. He was not concerned with consistency within a logical frame, with the rules of the game; he was concerned with how an idea "felt." He could, in a strangely devoted way, study science and seek out the great Jacques Loeb of the Rockefeller Institute, and at the same time wear a "health belt" and pay good money for sessions with a tea-leaf reader; consort with the New Masses crowd and at the same time write the pro-German Mencken "Hoch Hindenberg!" and drink to German victories; be a tourist attraction in Greenwich Village nightspots and at the same time brood back on the early years in Indiana. Mencken, who felt that the Dreiser of this period was wasting his time among the frauds of the Village, was right, at least in one sense, when he declared that Dreiser's "ideas always seem to be deduced from his feelings"; Mencken was right in that ideas that signified anything to Dreiser were absorbed into his own experience, were ingurgitated and assimilated with an innocent, uncritical voracity.

It is easy to sneer, as many critics yet sneer, at Dreiser as the uneducated yearner, the bumbling and pretentious back-street intellectual, the provincial autodidact; and sometimes the sneers, however uncharitable, are justified. But among the things that emerge from recent studies of Dreiser, especially the work of Ellen Moers, is the fact that Dreiser did not rest with the philosophical formulations of his masters from the nineteenth century, but constantly struggled to grasp what contemporary thought had to offer, and that he did hard and serious work, as when, under the guidance of Brill and Loeb, he tried to master and reconcile two of the great seminal ideas of the age, that of depth psychology and that of the study of the phenomena of life in terms of the laws of physics and chemistry.

This is not say that the impulse that drew Dreiser was the intellectual passion of the philosopher or scientist, or that the test of the validity of an idea was, for him, the philosopher's logic or the scientist's objective experiment. Rather, we may hazard that the impulse represented, at root, a need to make sense of the vast, amorphous puzzle that Theodore Dreiser was. The writings of fiction sprang, as we have indicated earlier, from the same need, and, in fact, the writing of fiction and the study of science and philosophy intertwine. For example, if we can say that, in the final sense, the needs of self-knowledge led Dreiser to Brill and Loeb, we must remember that, more immediately and specifically, Dreiser went to them for help in working toward *An American Tragedy*—which, in turn, summarized the long and complex struggle that his work represented. In this connection, looking ahead, we must emphasize that once *An American Tragedy* was written, Dreiser's mind moved more and more toward generalization and abstraction, and that all the unfriendly criticism of Dreiser as an intellectual becomes more and more to the point.

The fundamental fact is that for Dreiser ideas had to be absorbed into life, had to interpenetrate with experience, and had to do so in a massive fashion. This fact meant that ideas that, taken in abstraction, were mutually contradictory (as were those of Freud and Loeb or Marx) might be drawn with magisterial impartiality into a profound fiction like *An American Tragedy;* and in such a fiction, we may see, paradoxically, that the ideas do not interpret experience, experience interprets the ideas. The ideas have become merely the fuel of the creative passion, for only by creative passion could Dreiser discover what he really believed. He was almost as uncertain intellectually as he was unstable in love and friendship, and could be sure of an idea with only a little less difficulty than of his own feelings.* Like Cowperwood, he could not be sure of the difference between sincerity and the illusion of sincerity; as Randolph Bourne remarked of him, he had to "discover his own sincerity." Dreiser had only one way of doing that—by dramatization; and in this process the ideas absorbed into his bloodstream found their significance and their logic.

The period in the Village was for Dreiser one of floundering and groping for ideas, but it was also a period of confusion and change in his private life. Not only was there even greater complication and deceit in his innumerable sexual intrigues, but his relations with publishers became almost as confused and disingenuous. Dreiser was, apparently, incapable of sustaining a decent relationship with anyone. The role of friends, like that of mistresses, was to perform constant practical services with uncertain rewards, as typists, editors, agents, advertising and public relations experts, research assistants, lawyers, cooks, housemaids, and, no doubt, bootblacks. But the chief duty of a friend, as of a mistress or a publisher, was to feed the insatiable ego that, like the widow's womb, could never cry "Enough." Many friends came to understand him, usually all too well, but Mencken, devoted in friendship, seems to have understood him from the first. He said that Dreiser usually "played the fool"; that he "had an incurable antipathy for the *mot juste*" and an "insatiable appetite for the obviously not true"; and that the concept of gratitude was totally unavailable to his thought, much less to his feeling. But Mencken could feed that ego without stint, serve as critic, editor, and ballyhoo man, and say to friends that "we shall all be proud of having helped him." But all this meant nothing, when Mencken, though recognizing Dreiser's great stature, attacked *The "Genius."* In general, this was a time of ruptured friendships.

Two things did occur, however, to give some stability to Dreiser's life. First, a new publishing house, Boni and Liveright, sought Dreiser out with the hope of assembling his scattered literary properties under one roof. Second, there was a certain Helen Richardson, née Patges, who was twenty-five years old, very good-looking, a disappointed actress now working as a stenographer, and a second cousin of the novelist. On the strength of this kinship, Helen presented herself at his door, and two nights later was lyrically in his bed. For the rest of Dreiser's life, in spite of outrage on outrage, she was in and out of that bed, and in the end, in June 1944, he married her.

Now she wanted to go to Hollywood, and they went.

During this middle decade Dreiser's literary work, superficially at least, was as confused as the rest of his life. He had had a substantial advance for a projected novel, *The Bulwark,* but he could not get on with it, and when the advance was gone he was reduced to living from hand to mouth. He tried plays, which came to no good, a movie scenario, poems, numbers of short stories (which appeared in 1918 in a volume called *Free*), essays and articles, notably a philosophical piece, "Seeing the Universe," and upon entry of the United States into World War I, an ill-argued, ill-timed pro-German blast called "American Idealism and German

Frightfulness."* But the central concern of this period seems to have been a probing back into his own life. As early as 1914, before *The "Genius"* was in final form, Dreiser had seriously begun work on what was projected as a multi-volume autobiography, and by 1916, in the midst of his other occupations, he had finished the first volume, *Dawn*, which because of the revelations of the early lives of his sisters was not published until 1931. The second volume, *A Book About Myself*, was finished by 1919, but delayed in publication until 1922. Two other works of autobiographical importance belong to the period. In 1915, with Franklin Booth, another Indianian, Dreiser made a motor trip to revisit the scenes of his early days, including, of course, Terre Haute, there registering in the hotel where his mother had been a scrubwoman. Out of this trip came *A Hoosier Holiday*. Out of his long tangle of sexual adventures came *A Gallery of Women*, not published until 1929.

Looking back on these middle years, we can detect the emergence of a pattern. In *Sister Carrie* and *Jennie Gerhardt*, Dreiser, beginning his career in fiction, had written *out* of his life, but not *about* his life. These books were out of his life not only in that they embodied observed life and told the story of his sisters and family, but also in that they emphasized his deep obsessive concerns, the first novel in the story of failure-in-success and the second in the story of success-in-failure. Now, with the second period of his work, the concern with the self became more and more overt. In *The "Genius"* and the Trilogy, Dreiser is dealing with the dream-self—the superman, the success. In the autobiographical works, he is dealing, or trying to deal, with the literal self, whether success or failure; with the actual self, however that self may be evaluated. In the next phase, in *An American Tragedy*, he was to deal, not with the dream-self, but with the nightmare-self, the failure. Over the years he had been engaged in the long struggle to define the self and its contradictory potentialities—in the effort to "discover his own sincerity."

Meanwhile, in California, Helen made some success in the movies, playing, for instance, in Valentino's *Four Horsemen of the Apocalypse*, and by and large supported her lover. Even though his chemisms had begun to reassert themselves, she remained faithful to him. But his work on *The Bulwark* bogged down. New books, *Twelve Men, Hey, Rub-a-Dub-Dub*, and *The Color of a Great City*, had little success, and he had not published a novel since the ill-fated sex-saga of Witla.

Late in 1923, Dreiser, with the loyal Helen giving up her film future to accompany him, was back in New York, to face the literary gossip that he was finished as a writer. He was past fifty now, and a whole tribe of brilliant young novelists were springing up.

The making of *An American Tragedy* was a long process. As early as 1892, when he was a reporter on the St. Louis *Globe-Democrat*, Dreiser covered the murder of a girl who had died from eating poisoned candy provided by her sweetheart, and soon thereafter he began to collect clippings of similar cases—characteristically, the murder of a girl by a lover who aspires to a more advantageous match. One set of clippings concerned the case of a young man-about-town in New York, Roland Molineux, who in 1899 was indicted for the murder of a Mrs. Kate Adams. There was a certain irony in the case that must have pleased Dreiser, for Mrs. Adams was the victim only by accident; the poison, prepared by Roland, an amateur chemist, had been intended, apparently, for a fellow member of the Knickerbocker Athletic Club. Furthermore, it began to seem that Molineux had already poisoned another member, a rival in love. Strangely enough, it was this case, which bears little similarity to that of Clyde Griffiths in *An American Tragedy*, that set Dreiser to work on the general theme of his masterpiece, and there is evidence that he wrote some thirty chapters shortly after finishing *Sister Carrie*, but destroyed them.

In 1909, Dreiser wrote a story based on the case of a certain William Orphet, but by 1914 he returned to the Molineux case, perhaps with interest reawakened by the news of Molineux's death, in an asylum, of paresis. The new effort, called *The Rake* (or *The Moron*), was begun almost certainly late in 1914; the first sheet of the manuscript bears the address 165 West 10th Street, which Dreiser did not occupy until July of that year.* But Dreiser did not push this work very far, and began another novel based on the case of a young girl whose lover, a minister named Clarence Richesen, after getting a chance to rise in the world, with a post at Cambridge and an engagement to a socially prominent girl, killed his former sweetheart, who was pregnant and demanding. This project was abandoned too, and when, in 1919, Dreiser did return to his murder story, it was based on the case of young Chester Gillette, who had been convicted of murdering his pregnant sweetheart, a Grace ("Billie") Brown, back in 1906.

Thus we find that Dreiser began to collect the clippings in the early 1890's, when he was a struggling young outsider, and continued merely to collect them through the phase of his life when he had achieved some recognition as a journalist and was interviewing the great and the near-great for a magazine called *Success;* then, the first actual work began after 1900, when he balanced his first novels, concerned with girls who rise through sex from poverty and deprivation, by his morbid fascination with young men who, obsessed with sex and ambition, seize the way of murder to make their dreams come true.

But it would be a mistake to assume that the work toward *An American Tragedy* was continuous and imperative. Dreiser's general way of thinking does not give the impression that he would be characteristically focused on some one project and would stay with it to the end, but that some slow, grinding, general, all-inclusive life activity was going on, emerging now in one focus of interest and then in another. Even as late as 1920, Dreiser could promise Boni and Liveright (for what a promise from him to a publisher was worth) that a novel to be called *The Bulwark* would be finished by the end of the year.

In fact, in the period from the second attempt at *The Rake* to the publication of *An American Tragedy*, a little more than a decade, Dreiser was working on other novels, stories, plays, sketches, and the autobiographies. This was the general period when he seems to have been most deeply involved in thinking backward over his own life; and the poetry, for instance, is significant here not merely because of the content but because poetry had been his first form of composition, the original means by which he had come to realize himself and his world. It was out of this deep, slow, mulling process, by which Dreiser was trying to make sense of his own life, that the intuition of *An American Tragedy* drew to focus. When he did make a final commitment to his murder story, the particular story elected was one that had been collected years earlier.

Chester Gillette was the son of a fanatically devout couple who had run a slum mission. Born in the West, he had wound up, after two years at Oberlin College and much wandering, in Cortland, in upper New York. There an uncle owned a shirt factory, where Chester got a job and promptly seduced one of the girls employed there. Meanwhile, he had penetrated the world of "society" in Cortland. At this juncture Billie announced her pregnancy, and as her seducer withdrew into his more elegant life, she wrote him the letters that were to bring jurors to tears. With Billie insisting on marriage, Chester saw only one solution: he persuaded her to go on a trip with him, presumably to be married. At Big Moose Lake, he took her out in a rowboat. After he had hit her on the head with a tennis racket, she fell into the water and drowned. He left a straw hat (an extra provided for the occasion) to float on the water and announce his death, and fled the scene. He was captured, and in March, 1908, was executed.

The objective story of Chester is very close to that of Clyde, and Dreiser, rather than trying to disguise similarities, often insists on them. He keeps, for example, the initials of Chester Gillette for Clyde Griffiths, and the "B" of the nickname of Grace Brown for Bert, the nickname of Roberta Alden. For Clyde he keeps the pseudonym of Carl Graham, which Chester had used on the death trip with Billie. Big Moose Lake, where Billie died, becomes Big Bittern Lake. Chester's tennis racket (an improbable object for a jaunt in a rowboat) is transformed into a camera, but both items are accoutrements of a vacation. The family of Roberta, in its poverty and respectability, is like the Brown family

With only a little editing, the letters from Billie, which unstrung the jurors in the Herkimer County courthouse, become the letters of Roberta which unstring the jurors in the Cataraqui County courthouse.

Furthermore, Dreiser made a tour of the region where Chester had acted out his sleazy story. He saw the pushing little cities, the rutted roads and isolated farms, the very lake where, years back, Billie Brown had died, the dark woods into which Chester had fled, the Herkimer County courthouse, where Chester had been convicted. Dreiser heard the cry of the weir-weir bird that Chester must have heard and that Clyde was to hear. Dreiser could have changed all this; he could have used some setting he knew better, the Middle West, California,

Pittsburgh, or New York. But he did not. For one reason, his imagination fed on fact: this was where *it* had happened, and this was where *it* would now happen. Fact is doom, the ultimate, irreversible doom, and he was writing a story of doom.

For another reason, the factual scene was the proper laboratory in which the experiment of Clyde Griffiths' life could be performed in its purity. The town Lycurgus is a little node on a fringe filament of the great industrial society; the remoteness, the very smallness of scale, the triviality of the stakes being played for against the terrible cost of failure (or success), the contrast of the whole human project set against the lurking darkness of the primal woods and waters—all these factors give the action a kind of paradigmatic precision of outline and archetypal clarity of meaning. There is nothing to distract us from the logic of doom and the irony of the doom. The factual scene becomes, in Dreiser's imagination, the action: in its factuality it becomes, as the city had become in *Sister Carrie*, the image of doom, fulfilled and complete in the moment when Clyde, after the deed, disappears into the shadow of trees.

For *Sister Carrie* and *Jennie Gerhardt*, Dreiser had needed no file of clippings from old newspapers. The facts necessary for those novels needed no documentary validation; Dreiser's own experience and observation had validated them. Nor did *The "Genius"* need any documentary validation; for Dreiser was, in his own estimation, Eugene Witla. With the Trilogy, however, Dreiser had needed validation, for here he had to have the objective story into which his daydream-self, having no literally confirmatory memories, might enter. So with the nightmare-self. The nightmare-self needed the mystic mirror of the world of fact in order to have its story clear. Rather, Dreiser needed to understand the nature of the nightmare-self by brooding on a factual story which seemed to be a mirror, in order to elicit from his personal darkness of torturing potentiality the story lurking there.

The nightmare-self had long needed to find its story, for we know how far back goes the file of clippings. But so much had to be understood before Dreiser could make the final effort of self-understanding that would be *An American Tragedy*. There had to be the antithesis between the world of Carrie and that of Jennie. There had to be the long exploration of the autobiographies. There had to be the self-glorification in *The "Genius"* and the Trilogy. There had to be, perhaps, Dr. Brill with his gospel of the meaning of the past in the living self. In any case, Dreiser finally came into the time when he could recognize what the story of Chester Gillette really meant.

In an extremely interesting biographical-critical study called *The Two Dreisers*, Ellen Moers quotes Freud to the effect that a writer's subject is determined when "a strong experience in the present" awakens "a memory of an earlier experience . . . from which there now proceeds a wish which finds its fulfillment in the creative work." Applying this formula, Moers suggests that the "earlier experience" for Dreiser would have been his desire to get rid of his first wife Jug, and that the "strong experience in the present" would have been his falling in love with Helen Patges Richardson. But the first bloom of passion with Helen had scarcely passed before she, like Jug years back, began to pester him to marry her. Though Dreiser had long since got rid of Jug along with her nagging presence and her insatiable and burdensome sexuality, he had been lucky enough, or clever enough, to do so, not by a divorce but by a legal separation, thus converting the old liability into a new asset: a protection against future matrimony. *Plus ça change* . . . If Helen was to get her way in the end, that end was a long time coming, only, in fact, a little more than a year before Dreiser's death, when Jug's death had removed, willy-nilly, the happy legal impediment and age had reduced Dreiser's powers of resistance.

Meanwhile, just back from California, at work on *An American Tragedy,* and in good health, Dreiser had moved out on Helen, now seeing her only as it suited his pleasure or convenience, in a sort of stopgap or backstop way. He did, however, take the devoted but demanding lady on the tour of upper New York, where Chester had taken Billie on the fatal honeymoon, and where Clyde was to take Roberta. In his passion for factuality, Dreiser even went for a row with Helen on Big Moose Lake. During the little outing, she reflected: "Maybe Teddy will become completely hypnotized by this idea and even repeat it, here and now." Helen was never very astute; if she had any need to fear, it was not because her lover was hypnotized by a literary notion, it was because she had cast herself in the role of the female victim that Dreiser's secret drama always demanded.

It was this secret drama that Dreiser was now undertaking to reenact in his imagination. He was not, in fact, trying to put himself imaginatively in the place of Chester or Clyde. He was not, in the end, trying to tell their story. He was trying to tell his own, and his own story had begun long before he ever heard of either Jug or Helen.

Dreiser told that story in *Dawn*—there the murder story without the murder. This is the story of his own growing up, the deprived one, the yearner, the quester. At the very end of *Dawn*, when the young Dreiser has entered into the temptations of the world, has committed fornication and has dared to enter the glitter of a real restaurant, we find, as a summary of his life thus far, the following self-portrait:

> I have to smile. Poor, cocky, hungry, without the faintest notion of the deeps of luxury, expenditure, control, taste, here I was, assuming that I was reasonably near if not well within the gates! And at the same time, nervous as to the impending ills of a rake!

It is a strange phrase: "the impending ills of a rake." In the first place, the word *rake* does not occur (unless I have missed it) elsewhere in the autobiographies. We know that Dreiser did know the cautionary tales of harlot and rake and idle apprentice illustrated in Hogarth's work (even if, in the autobiography, he transfers Hogarth from his eighteenth century back to the reign of Charles II), and it is possible that he made some connection between Hogarth's grim warnings and his own account of the doom of a rake; and almost certainly the mature author of *Dawn*, looking back with pity and condescension on the poor, cocky, hungry boy, identified him, by the word *rake*, with the hero of the murder stories he had collected and was to collect.

But what were the "impending ills of a rake"? In *Dawn* this passage introduced the tale of the embezzlement of twenty-five dollars to buy the fashionable overcoat necessary for a rake, and the loss of a good job. But the loss of a job or even a jail sentence is, we know, only the beginning of the ills of a rake: at the end waits the gallows or the chair. All the stories of the rake are murder stories, and the victim is always the trusting maid who loves not wisely but too well; and the common theme is the murder of love for gain and ambition. And that is the theme of the personal story of the young Dreiser up through *A Book About Myself*, which ends with the marriage to Jug—"after the first flare of love had thinned down to the pale flame of duty."

The tale had begun, it should be emphasized, long before Dreiser ever laid eyes on Jug; Jug enters the tale, but she enters fairly late and does not provide, in any exclusive sense, the "earlier experience" that Miss Moers would emphasize. First, there is the boy "blazing with sex," masturbating and tortured by fear of "imaginary sex weakness." Next, there is the episode of the nameless little "reckless and adventure-looking Italian girl of not more than sixteen or seventeen," who in "an idle or adventuring mood" comes into the real-estate office where the boy is alone for the afternoon, and lures or badgers him into the back room, where he finally musters up enough courage to make love to her on an old couch abandoned there. At the moment when she clutches him "convulsively and even affectionately" and then lies back in "a smiling calm," his life is changed. He knew, he says in *Dawn*, that now he *"could* hold this relationship with a normal, healthy girl," and looked forward to "all the others" with whom he "might come into intimate and affectionate relationship—a grand programme." So the pattern of his life is set—a pattern over which, we may surmise, always presided the archetypal figure of the girl who, as though summoned by a dream, comes out of nowhere to give herself to him and, after the spasm and the moment of smiling calm, disappears into nowhere, nameless and undemanding.*

In this third phase, at the same time that the boy Dreiser, presumably freed from the fears of impotence,** is seeking sex, he has the "giddy dreams" of the world of wealth, elegance, social position, and ostentation. As a laundry boy making deliveries at rich houses in Chicago, Dreiser had yearned, just as Carrie does on her timid expedition to the Shore Drive, to penetrate into those mansions where happiness was the rule of life, and had peered through doorways "into boudoirs and reception rooms," to catch "flashy touches of social superiority and social supremacy," and could vision himself "in golden chambers," giving himself "over to what luxuries and delights." He longed to "succeed financially by marriage with some beautiful and wealthy girl," but he never met the dream girl who was both "sensual" and "rich."

What he met was little Nellie MacPherson, behind the cashier's desk in the laundry. She was pretty, gay, good-natured, quick at repartee, and sweet, but she was "embedded in a conservative and wholly religious family —Scotch Presbyterian"—as he was to find Jug embedded in her Missouri Methodism. In any case, Nellie was not the girl Dreiser would have chosen from the "veritable garden of femininity" that the laundry room was.* She was merely what he, in his limitations, had to make do with. The best he could do was to act out the charade of a love affair with her, and go regularly to her house where he basked in the respect and admiration of her family, where he secretly preferred the younger sister, where he spent endless hours cuddling Nellie and talking of their married bliss to come and systematically trying to seduce her. Though she was not "lustful" like the nameless little Italian girl, she was "passionate enough within her conventional tether," and now and then he almost "over-ran her good judgment." He had no intention of marrying her. His vainglorious ambitions lay elsewhere, even in the realm of intellectual achievement, and in *Dawn*, like Cowperwood looking back with pity on the "passionate illusion" of Aileen's girlhood love for him, Dreiser could write:

> I think I must have been her first serious affair. The pity of it was that she had no understanding of the type of youth she was dealing with, any more than I had of myself, and soon believed in the gushing phrases I lavished upon her.

It was all a charade.

But even as Dreiser lavished the "gushing phrases" on Nellie, he was trying them out on Alice, and thus begins the pattern of the double (or multiple) romance which was to continue for Dreiser's life, and which is the central fact of the story of Clyde. With Alice, who begins *A Book About Myself*, Dreiser repeated all the protracted deceptions and self-deceptions of planning for marriage, the reveling imaginary bliss to come, the various gambits of seduction he had become acquainted with.

He had been resentful of Nellie because, in spite of the "white tenseness" of her face and her "almost savage embraces," she would not surrender to him, but with Alice there was, in the end, another kind of resentment. Once she "in her own home threw some pillows on the floor," and lay down and begged him to "love" her. Later Dreiser could write of the event: "I fancy she thought that if she yielded to me physically and found herself with child my sympathy would cause me to marry her." But she had mistaken her man; he thought it "wise" not to oblige her. In fact, there was no way for a Nellie or an Alice to win, neither by fending off this lover nor by surrendering to him.

When at last Dreiser left Alice, whom he had cunningly not deflowered, he went to St. Louis to a better newspaper job, and the letter she wrote him there had all the pathos of those of Billie Brown, or Roberta Alden. Dreiser, suffering loneliness, remorse, and self-pity, wrote her that he loved her and that her letter had torn his heart. But in looking back on that moment, he says, in *A Book About Myself*, of his own letter: "But I could not write it as effectually as I might have, for I was haunted by the idea that I should never keep my word. Something kept telling me that it was not wise, that I didn't really want to."

The "something" was always there, pronouncing his doom. He yearned for love, but only, as he put it, "after I had the prosperity and fame that somehow I falsely fancied commanded love." If he was "blazing with sex," he was also blazing with the "desire for material and social supremacy—to have wealth, to be in society." That "something" was the voice of the anguishingly uncertain ego that had to have "prosperity and fame" before it could feel itself even to exist—or if existing, to be worthy of love. And the voice was so cold and commanding that it seemed to be the very voice of destiny. The voice, for Dreiser and for Clyde in the great scene of the temptation to murder Roberta, when the Efrit speaks to him, seemed detached from the self, and this fact exculpated the self. And the same exculpation is also here when, in *A Book About Myself*, the self looks at the self:

> I saw myself a stormy petrel hanging over the yellowish-black waves of life and never really resting anywhere. I could not; my mind would not let me. I saw too much, felt too much, knew too much. What I, what anyone, but a small bit of seaweed on an endless sea, flotsam, jetsam, being moved hither and thither—by what subterranean tides?*

By what subterranean tides? That is the question underlying *An American Tragedy*.

By the same token that Dreiser can exculpate the self as a victim of subterranean tides, he can pity the self; and in the next stage, he can pity and bless the girl whom he would take as victim—Alice ("She wanted to unite with me for this little span of existence, to go with me hand in hand into the ultimate nothingness"), or Nellie, or Roberta, none of whom could understand the grip of subterranean tides.

There is, however, another stage in the natural history of pity. In *A Book About Myself*, at the end of the paragraph from which I have quoted the sentence on "prosperity and fame," Dreiser says: ". . . at the same time I was horribly depressed by the thought that I should never have them [prosperity, fame, love], never; and that thought, for the most part has been fulfilled." But after this self-pity, in the next paragraph, in the very next sentence, we find:

> In addition to this, I was filled with an intense sympathy for the woes of others, life in all its helpless degradation and poverty, the unsatisfied dreams of people, their sweaty labors, the things they were compelled to endure—nameless impositions, curses, brutalities,—the things they would never have, their hungers, half-formed dreams of pleasure, their gibbering insanities and beaten resignations at the end.

This paragraph continues with a Whitmanesque catalog of human sufferings and Dreiser's confession of the literal tears that we must believe he shed. But then the next two paragraphs return to the young man's preoccupation with his own defects and limitations, his obsessive fear of failure, his yearning looks into the house of "some kindly family" or through the "windows of some successful business firm" and his "aches and pains that went with all this, the amazing depression, all but suicidal."

In *Dawn* and in the first twenty-two chapters of *A Book About Myself*, not only the basic personality and life pattern of Dreiser himself have been presented and analyzed, but the basic characters, situations, and issues of *An American Tragedy* have been projected. All is ready. Life is there, ready for the understanding that will make art possible and the art that will make understanding possible. And at the end of this period Dreiser had even begun to write poems and had become friends with a newspaperman who had written a "Zolaesque" novel.

But there was to be an essential, intermediate stage in the progress toward *An American Tragedy*. Up to this moment, the elements that were to reappear in Dreiser's great masterpiece, and indeed, in his fiction in general, had been floating, not brought to focus in experience. The entrance of Sara White—poor Jug, who could not understand the subterranean tides—was to do this. Her presence dominates the second half of *A Book About Myself*, and brings to focus all that had been diffused in Dreiser's experience; and the key episode occurs when a newspaperman, seeing the photograph of the twenty-two-year-old Dreiser's fiancée, declares that if he marries such a "conventional and narrow woman," and one older to boot, he'll be gone. He gives further advice: "Run with the girls if you want, but don't marry." Looking back on this moment, Dreiser wrote:

> She would never give herself to me without marriage, and here I was, lonely and financially unable to take her, and spiritually unable to justify my marriage to her even if I were. The tangle of life, its unfairness and indifference to the moods and longings of any individual, swept over me once more, weighing me down far beyond the power of expression.

Life's "unfairness and indifference to the moods

and longings of any individual": the generalization of pity in the phrase "of any individual" is a mask for the self-pity. The whole phrase should be revised to read: *Life's unfairness and indifference to the moods and longings of Theodore Dreiser—or Clyde Griffiths.* Thus we sense the implied premise: *The moods and longings of Theodore Dreiser—or of Clyde Griffiths—are the measure of justice.* And from this premise flows the inexorable conclusion: *Those who would contravene these sacred moods and longings shall have justice visited upon them.*

Poor Jug. Poor Roberta.

*A*n *American Tragedy* is the work in which Dreiser could look backward from the distance of middle age and evaluate his own experience of success and failure. We feel, in this book, the burden of the personal pathos, the echo of the personal struggle to purge the unworthy aspirations, to discover his own sincerity. We also feel, in this book, the burden of a historical moment, the moment of the Great Boom which climaxed the period from Grant to Coolidge, the half-century in which the new America of industry and finance capitalism was hardening into shape and its secret forces were emerging to dominate all life. In other words, *An American Tragedy* can be taken as a document, both personal and historical, and it is often admired, and defended, in these terms.

As a document, it is indeed powerful, but such documentary power is derivative: an artifact dug from the Sumerian tomb moves us not because it is beautiful but because some human hand, nameless and long since dust, had fashioned it; and a book may move us because we know what, of a man's life or of a moment in history, it represents. But the power of *An American Tragedy* is not derivative. The weight of Dreiser's experience and that of the historical moment are here, but they are here as materials; in the strange metabolism of creation, they are absorbed and transmuted into fictional idea, fictional analogy, fictional illusion. The book is "created," and therefore generates its own power, multiplying the power implicit in the materials.

The thing in *An American Tragedy* most obviously created is Clyde Griffiths himself. The fact that Dreiser, in his characteristic way, chose a model for Clyde does not make Clyde less of a creation. Rather, it emphasizes that he is a creation; and the contrast between the dreary factuality of an old newspaper account and the anguishing inwardness of the personal story may well have served as a mirror for the contrast that always touched Dreiser's feelings and fired his imagination— the contrast between the grinding impersonality of the machine of the world and the pathos of the personal experience. In fact, the novel begins and ends with an image of this contrast: the family of street preachers, in the beginning with the boy Clyde and in the end with the illegitimate son of Clyde's sister Esta, stand lost between the "tall walls of the commercial heart of an American city" and lift up their hymn "against the vast skepticism and apathy of life." The image of the boy Clyde looking up at the "tall walls" of the world is the key image of the novel. And of Dreiser's life.

The creation of the character of Clyde is begun by

a scrupulous accretion of detail, small indications, and trivial events. We are early caught in the dawning logic of these details. We early see the sidewise glances of yearning—the yearning he later feels when staring at the rich house of his uncle, and again when for the first time he lays eyes on Sondra, with "a curiously stinging sense of what it was to want and not to have." We see how, when he discovers his sister Esta in the secret room, his first reaction is selfish; how only when she refers to "poor Mamma" does his own sympathy stir; how this sympathy is converted suddenly into a sense of world-pathos, and then, in the end, turns back into self-pity. We see his real sadness at Roberta's jealousy, which he, also one of the deprived, can feel himself into, but we know that his pity for her is, at root, self-pity. We see him open the *Times-Union* to see the headline: *Accidental Double Tragedy at Pass Lake*. We see all this, and so much more, and remember his mother's letter to him after his flight from Kansas City: "...for well I know how the devil tempts and pursues all of us mortals, and particularly just such a child as you." And what a stroke it is to fuse the reader's foreboding interest with the anxiety of the mother!

For Dreiser's method of presenting the character is far deeper and more subtle than that of mere accretion. The method is an enlargement and a clarifying, slow and merciless, of a dimly envisaged possibility. We gradually see the inward truth of the mother's clairvoyant phrase, "such a child as you"; and the story of Clyde is the documentation of this.

A thousand strands run backward and forward in

this documentation, converting what is a process in time into a logic outside of time. When, back in Kansas City, we see Clyde's sexual fear and masochism in relation to the cold, cunning Hortense, we are laying the basis for our understanding of what will come later, the repetition with Sondra of the old relationship and the avenging of it on the defenseless Roberta. When, in the room of women where Clyde is foreman, he looks wistfully out the window on the summer river, we are being prepared for the moment when he first encounters Roberta at the pleasure lake, and for the grimmer moment to come on Big Bittern Lake. When, on the night after the first meeting with Sondra, Clyde does not go to Roberta, we know that this is a shadowy rehearsal for the last betrayal and murder.

It is not only that we find, in an analytic sense, the logic of character displayed; in such instances we find this logic transliterated into a thousand intermingling images, and in this transliteration the logic itself becoming the poetry of destiny. We see the process moving toward climax when, on the train, on the death ride with Roberta, Clyde flees from his own inner turmoil into the objective observations which, in their irrelevancy, are the mark of destiny: *Those nine black and white cows on that green hillside*, or *Those three automobiles out there running almost as fast as the train*. And we find the climax of the process in the "weird, contemptuous, mocking, lonely" call of the weir-weir bird which offers a commentary on the execution, as it had on the birth, of the murderous impulse.

This transliteration of logic into a poetry of destiny

is what accounts for our peculiar involvement in the story of Clyde. What man, short of saint or sage, does not understand, in some secret way however different from Clyde's way, the story of Clyde and does not find it something deeper than a mere comment on the values of American culture? Furthermore, the mere fact that our suspense is not about the *what* but about the *how* and the *when* emphasizes our involvement. No, to be more specific, our *entrapment*. We are living out a destiny, painfully waiting for a doom. We live into Clyde's doom, and in the process live our own secret sense of doom which is the backdrop of our favorite dramas of the will.

The depth of our involvement—or entrapment—is indicated by the sudden sense of lassitude, even release, once the murder is committed; all is now fulfilled, and in that fact the drawstring is cut. With the act thus consummated, we may even detach ourselves, at least for the moment, from the youth now "making his way through a dark, uninhabited wood, a dry straw hat upon his head, a bag in his hand. . . ."

As a commentary of Dreiser's art, we can note how, after this sentence that closes Book II, Dreiser jerks back his camera from that lonely figure and begins Book III by withdrawing into magisterial distance for a panoramic sweep of the lens: "Cataraqui County extending from the northernmost line of the village known as Three Mile Bay on the south to the Canadian border, on the north a distance of fifty miles. . . . Its greatest portion covered by uninhabited forests and. . . ." The whole effect is that of detachment; and with this we are restored, after a long painful while, to the role of observer, interested and critical, but not now involved.

But we shall not be long permitted to keep this comfortable role. Soon the camera will come close to the cell where Clyde waits, the focus will be sharpened. And in this constant alternation of focus, and shift from involvement to detachment, we find one of the deep art-principles of the work, one of the principles of its compelling rhythm. It is compelling because the shift of focus is never arbitrary; it grows out of the expressive needs of the narrative as Dreiser has conceived it, and out of the prior fact that the narrative is conceived as a drama involving both the individual and the universe.

Randolph Bourne once said that Dreiser had the "artist's vision without the sureness of the artist's technique." This is true of much of Dreiser's work, and in a limited sense may be true of *An American Tragedy*. I have used the phrase "Dreiser's art" in full awareness that most critics, even critics as dangerous to disagree with as Lionel Trilling, will find it absurd; and in full awareness that even those who admire Dreiser will, with few exceptions, concede a point on "art," or apologetically explain that Dreiser's ineptitudes somehow have the value of stylistic decorum and can be taken as a manifestation of his groping honesty, and will then push on to stake their case on his "power" and "compassion."

But ultimately how do we know the "power" or the "compassion"—know them differently, that is, from the power or compassion we may read into a news story—except by Dreiser's control? Except, in other words, by the rhythmic organization of his materials, the vibrance which is the life of fictional illusion, the tension among elements, and the mutual interpenetration in meaning of part and whole which gives us the sense of preternatural fulfillment? Except, in short, by art?

There is a tendency to freeze the question of Dreiser as an artist at the question of prose style. As for prose style, Dreiser is a split writer. There is the "literary" writer whose style is often abominable. But there is another writer, too, a writer who can create a scene with fidelity if not always with felicity. But often there is felicity, a felicity of dramatic baldness: the letters of Mrs. Griffiths or Roberta; the scene of Roberta back home, in her mother's house, looking out at the ruined fields; the scene when Clyde first sees Sondra, with that "curiously stinging sense of what it is to want and not to have"; the whole sequence leading up to the murder.

Words are what we have on the page of a novel, and words are not only a threshold, a set of signs, but indeed a fundamental aspect of meaning, absorbed into everything else. Words, however, are not the only language of fiction. There is the language of the unfolding scenes, what Dreiser, in the course of composing the novel, called the "procession and selection of events," the language of the imagery of enactment, with all its primitive massiveness—the movie in our heads, with all the entailed questions of psychological veracity and subtlety, of symbolic densities and rhythmic complexities. I am trying here to indicate something of the weight of this language, or better, these languages, as an aspect of Dreiser's art.*

With this intention we can return to the question of the rhythm between detachment and involvement, which manifests itself in shifts of pace and scale. But we may find the basis for another rhythm in the fact that the personal story of Clyde is set in a whole series of shifting perspectives that generate their own rhythm. By perspective I do not mean a point of view in the ordinary technical sense. I mean what may be called an angle of interest. For instance, the picture of the organization of the collar factory in Lycurgus gives a perspective on life, and on the fate of Clyde; this is another contrast between mechanism and man, a symbolic rendering of the ground-idea of the novel that with each new perspective is re-introduced at rhythmic intervals.

But there are many perspectives. There is the perspective of the religious belief of the family, which returns in the end to frame the whole story; that of the world of the bellhop's bench in the hotel; that of sex and "chemism"; that of the stamping room in the factory with its mixture of sex, social differences, power, and money; that of the economic order of Lycurgus which stands as a mirror for the world outside; that of the jealousies and intrigues of the young social set of the town, jealousies and intrigues which, ironically enough, make it possible for Clyde to enter that charmed circle; that of justice and law in relation to the political structure of Cataraqui County; that of the death house.

Sometimes a perspective comes as an idea boldly stated, sometimes as implicit in a situation or person. In fact, all the persons of the novel, even the most incidental, are carriers of ideas and represent significant perspectives in which the story may be viewed. In the enormous cast there are no walk-ons; each actor has a role in the structure of the unfolding dialectic. And it is the pervasive sense of this participation, however unformulated, that gives the novel its density, the weight of destiny.

If, as a matter of fact, the dialectic were insisted upon merely as dialectic, we should not find this weight; and this is the great difference between the method of *An American Tragedy* and that of the Trilogy. In *An American Tragedy* the dialectic unfolds in personality, in the presentation of personality not as a carrier of an idea but as a thing of inner vibrance. The mother, for instance, is a small masterpiece of characterization. She is the carrier of "religion," but with her own inner contradictions, exists in her full and suffering reality, a reality which, at the end when she comes to join Clyde, affirms itself by her effect on everyone around. Roberta is fully rendered, not only in her place in the social and economic order and in her role as victim, but with the complexity of her humanity. When her friend Grace catches her in a lie about Clyde, she stiffens with "resentment," and this conversion of her self-anger into the relief of anger at her friend is a telling index, given in a flash, of the depth and anguish of her scarcely formulated inner struggle. She does not quite tell the truth to her mother about why she moves out of her first room. In the midst of her as yet submerged moral struggle, she deceives even herself as to why she selects a room downstairs and with an outside door in the new house. She is a sufferer, but she is not beyond the flash of jealous

‡ *120* ‡

anger when Clyde, with unconscious brutality, remarks that Sondra dresses well: "If I had as much money as that, I could too." And the scene in which Clyde tries to persuade her to let him come to her room is of extraordinary depth, coming to climax when he turns sullenly away, and she, overwhelmed by the fear and pain at her own rebelliousness, feels the "first, flashing, blinding, bleeding stab of love."

Even minor characters have more than their relation to the dialectic. The prosecuting attorney and the defending lawyers have their own depths, and their roles are defined by their personal histories. A character like Hortense may be merely sketched in, but she takes on a new significance when we see her, like Rita, as an earlier image of Sondra, who is—and let us dwell on the adjectives—"as smart and vain and sweet a girl as Clyde had ever laid eyes on." And if at first Sondra herself seems scarcely more than another example of the particular type of *femme fatale* destined to work Clyde's ruin, let us remember how Clyde, in his cell, receives the letter beginning: "Clyde—This is so that you will not think someone once dear to you has utterly forgotten you. . . ." The letter, typewritten, is unsigned, but with it, in all the mixture of human feeling and falsity, Sondra, retroactively as it were, leaps to life.

As every person enters the story with a role in the dialectic, so every person enters with a human need which seeks fulfillment in the story. The delineation of this need—for instance, the portrait of the socially ambitious clerk in Lycurgus or the history of the prosecuting attorney Mason—serves to distract our interest from

Clyde's personal story, to provide another kind of distancing of the main line of narrative. At the same time, in the extraordinary coherence of the novel, we finally see that such apparent digressions are really mirrors held up to Clyde's story, in fact to Clyde himself: in this world of mirrors complicity is the common doom. So here we have another version, in distraction of interest and realization of complicity, of the rhythm of approach and withdrawal.

There is, indeed, another sense in which the delineation of each new need compensates, in the end, for the distraction it has provoked. Each new need introduced into the novel serves as a booster to the thrust of narrative, each providing a new energy that, though at first a distraction, is absorbed into the central drive; and in the rhythm of these thrusts, we find another principle of the organization of the whole. Or to change our image, in the braiding together of these needs with the need of Clyde, we find a rhythm of pause and acceleration, the pulse of creative life.

To put the matter in another way, the delineation of each new perspective, each new person, each new need, serves as a new analysis of the dynamism of the story; for instance, the psychological make-up of the prosecutor, his frustrations and yearnings, are a part of the explanation of the course of justice. Each new element reveals a new depth of motive; there is a progressive "unmasking" of the secret springs of the action, related in the end to the "unmasking" of life as a mechanism cursed with consciousness, and something of our own resistance to unmasking enters into the whole response to the story. This resistance, set against our natural commitment to the narrative, creates another sort of tension, and another sort of rhythm of withdrawal and approach. Furthermore, over against the unmasking of the mechanism of life is set the feel of life itself being lived in the urgency of its illusions; and the play between the elements of this contrast gives us another principle of rhythm, another principle by which the form unfolds.

I have spoken of the marked moment of withdrawal at the beginning of Book III, after we have left Clyde walking away from the scene of Roberta's death, into the forest. Our commitment to the movement of narrative leading to the death of Roberta has been so complete that now, with the death accomplished, the story of the crime seems, for the moment at least, to split off from the subsequent story of consequences; and Dreiser, by the moment of withdrawal into distance, emphasizes the split. The split, coming about two thirds of the way through the novel, has been felt, by some readers, to be a grave flaw in the structure. The split is indeed real—a real break in emotional continuity. But we must ask ourselves whether or not this split serves, as the similar "split" in Conrad's *Lord Jim* or Shakespeare's *Julius Caesar*, to emphasize a deeper thematic continuity.

The story is one of crime and consequences. In the first two Books we see the forces that converge toward the death of Roberta, and in Book III we see the forces that are triggered into action by her death; that is, we see the relation of the individual personality, and individual fate, to such forces as a continuing theme. But there is another and more general principle of continuity. The world in which the crime occurs is one of shadowy complicities, where all things seem to conspire in evil; the shadowiness of the outer world is matched by the shadowiness of the inner world. In such a world, what is the nature of responsibility? For instance, is Clyde really responsible for Roberta's death? At the very last moment in the boat he does not "will" to strike her—her death is an "accident." This "accident," to which we must return, ends Book II, but in the sequel the theme of responsibility and complicity are developed more fully and subtly, and the shadowiness of the inner world merges again and again with that of the outer. For instance, Jephson, one of the lawyers defending Clyde, creates a new version of the accident; and then Clyde is persuaded, without much resistance, to testify to a "lie" in order to establish, as Jephson puts it, the "truth."

This scene of the "persuasion" of Clyde is balanced by a later scene in which, after Clyde's conviction, the young preacher McMillan strips Clyde of all his lies, alibis, and equivocations, and prepares him for repentance and salvation; in other words, McMillan asserts the idea of responsibility. But just before the execution, even as Clyde assures his mother that God has heard his prayers, he is asking himself: "Had he?" And Clyde goes to his death not knowing what he really thinks or feels, or what he has done. This theme of ambiguity—of complicity and responsibility—runs in varying manifestations through the novel; Clyde has always lived in the ambiguous mists of dream, and the most important thing shrouded from his sight is his own identity. In a world of shadowy complicities and uncertain responsibility, what is identity?

At the end, on death row, there is a little episode that asserts again the theme of identity in the novel. One of the condemned awaiting death is a man named Nicholson, a lawyer who has poisoned a client to gain control of his estate. Nicholson is clearly a man of breeding and education, and in spite of his criminality, has courage, humor, kindliness, and dignity. In short, he has a self that can somehow survive his own criminality and its consequences. His role in the story is a thematic one. He is set in contrast to Clyde—who has no "self"—and undertakes to instruct him in the rudimentary dignity of having an identity. When he is to be executed, he sends two books to Clyde, *Robinson Crusoe* and *The Arabian Nights*.

Here we find repeated the little device with which Dreiser indicates his meaning when he gives us the last glimpse of Carrie, sitting in her rocking chair with a copy of *Père Goriot* on her lap, the study of another "little soldier of fortune." As the novel of Balzac, whose fiction long ago had made Dreiser aware of his own role as the "ambitious beginner," so the gifts of Nicholson summarize the theme of *An American Tragedy*. The two books provide the poles of Clyde's story.

The significance of *Robinson Crusoe* is clear. It gives the image of a man who is totally self-reliant, who, alone and out of nothing, can create a life for himself, a world. Even in shipwreck—in disaster—he asserts and fulfills the self (as, we may say, Nicholson does).

As for *The Arabian Nights,* Dreiser does not have to trust the reader for a last-minute interpretation. At the trial, while Jephson is leading Clyde in his testimony, we find the following passage:

> "I see! I see!" went on Jephson, oratorically and loudly, having the jury and audience in mind. "A case of the Arabian Nights, of the enscorcelled and the enscorcellor [*sic*]."
>
> "I don't think I know what you mean," said Clyde.
>
> "A case of being bewitched, my poor boy—by beauty, love, wealth, by things that we sometimes think we want very, very much, and cannot ever have—that is what I mean, and that is what much of the love in the world amounts to."

In this passage Jephson summarizes the whole story of Clyde, but the summary has long since been prepared for in the novel. At the very beginning of his worldly career, in his "imaginary flights," the hotel where he was a bellhop seemed a magic world, "Aladdinish, really": "It meant that you did what you pleased." And this Aladdinish world, where dream is law, appears again at the very crucial moment of the novel when Clyde is being tempted by the genie, or Efrit, to the murder of Roberta:

> Indeed the center or mentating section of his brain at this time might well have been compared to a sealed and silent hall in which alone and undisturbed, and that in spite of himself, he now sat thinking on the mystic or evil and terrifying desires or advice of some darker or primordial and unregenerate nature of his own, and without the power to drive the same forth or himself to decamp, and yet also without the courage to act upon anything.
>
> For now the genii of his darkest and weakest side

was speaking. And it said: "And would you escape from the demands of Roberta that but now and unto this hour have appeared unescapable to you? Behold! I bring you a way. It is the way of the lake—Pass Lake. This item that you have read—do you think it was placed in your hands for nothing?

Notice that the genie's argument involves the notion that all is "done for" Clyde without his stir: the newspaper with the story of the death at Pass Lake has not been "placed" in his hands "for nothing." And this, of course, echoes Dreiser's analysis of his own need to have things "done for him"— which we shall come to shortly. Furthermore, we again notice here the situation of the self regarding the self, and the exculpation of self.

This is the world where dream is law and every wish is fulfilled effortlessly and innocently. The first Aladdinish dream, back in the Green-Davidson in Kansas City, had merely been to be like the guests of the hotel: "That you possessed all of these luxuries. That you went how, where, and when you pleased." * Now the dream is different and dire; but the Efrit is ready still to show how it may be gratified, effortlessly and innocently, as in a dream. And the theme of the Aladdinish dream is merely a variant of the theme of identity—if wishes come true without responsibility, the moral meaning of the self is denied.**

The fact that Dreiser divides the novel into only three Books falsifies the intrinsic structure and blurs the fundamental theme. There are really four basic movements of the narrative, and there should be four Books: the story up to the flight from Kansas City, that of the preparation; the story of the temptation leading to the death of Roberta; the story of the conviction, that of the ambiguities of justice; and the story of the search, as death draws near, for salvation and certainty as contrasted with ambiguity. In other words, the present Book III should be divided; and then in the latter half, related to other themes, especially to that of Aladdin, but more deeply grounded, the theme of identity would be specific and dominant.

Throughout the whole novel this theme has been emerging. If in the world of complicities and ambiguities, it is hard to understand responsibility, then how, ultimately, can one understand the self? If one's dream is to "have things done for you," if one is passive, how can there be a self? In fact, in this world of shadows Clyde has always sought to flee from the self. In all his self-absorption and selfishness, he has sought to repudiate the deepest meaning of self. He had longed to enter the "tall walls" of the world and find there a dream-self, a self-to-be-created, a role to play in the rich and thrilling world—a *role*, we may say, to take the place of a *self*. The very end of Book I, which has described Clyde's first attempt to enter the world, shows him fleeing from the wreck of the borrowed car: ". . . he hoped to hide—to lose himself and so escape. . . ." He wishes to escape responsibility and punishment; he does "lose himself," and early in Book II we learn that he has lost his name, to reassume it only when he can use it to advantage with his rich uncle from Lycurgus.

All the rest of the story can be regarded as an attempt to repudiate the old self. And the repudiation of self is associated with Clyde's readiness to repudiate others: he is ashamed of his family; he drops new friends—Dillard and Rita, for example—as soon as he makes contact with his rich relations; he ends by murdering Roberta. Or it may be put that Clyde, having no sense of the reality of self, has no sense of the reality of others; for instance, when Clyde assists Roberta into the boat that is to take her to her death, she seems "an almost nebulous figure . . . stepping down into an unsubstantial rowboat, upon a purely ideational lake." And as we have found earlier, even his pity for others is always a covert self-pity or a pity for the self that could not be, truly, a self.

At the end, in a last desperate hope, Clyde is forced by McMillan to recognize the truth that he has fled from responsibility and self. But even now, as Clyde tries to recognize this fact and thus discover and accept a self, he cannot be sure of who or what he is. His "tragedy" is that of namelessness, and this is one aspect of its being an American tragedy, the story of the individual without identity, whose responsible self has been absorbed by the great machine of modern industrial secularized society, and reduced to a cog, a cipher, an abstraction.* Many people, including Sergei Eisenstein, who in his scenario, for a film that was never made, presents Clyde as the mere victim of society, have emphasized the social determinism in *An American Tragedy*, and James Farrell, in an essay on *Sister Carrie*, in *The League of Frightened Philistines*, succinctly summarizes this view:

To him [Dreiser] evil is social: all his novels are concerned with social history, the social process of evil. Ambition, yearning, aspiration—these all revolve around this problem, and it in turn revolves around the role of money. He has related social causation . . . to the individual pattern of destiny.

It is one of the great achievements of Dreiser that he grasped and dramatized American urban society more strongly than any other writer. He did indeed relate social causation to the individual pattern of destiny, but deeper than this story of the individual set against the great machine of secularized society, is the story of the individual set against the great machine of the universe —the story we find in the image of Cowperwood, in prison, staring up at the stars, or in that of Clyde, after the death of Roberta, moving into the darkness of the woods. Furthermore, the contrast of man set against the universe is no more a complete description of his fate than that of man set against society. For man is not merely set against the machine of society or of the universe; he is himself a machine, and is set against the machine that is himself.

This was the doctrine that Dreiser, in the years leading up to *An American Tragedy*, adapted from Jacques Loeb, one of the pioneers in establishing the explanation of life by physicochemical laws subject to exploration by the methods of the laboratory.* Under the tutelage of Loeb, Dreiser had come to feel that the stars that are indifferent to man, or would cross him, are not in the sky but in his bloodstream and nerve cells and genes; and that man himself is the dark wood in which he wanders. And this brings us back to Dreiser's theme of illusion.

‡ *130* ‡

Success, power, place, wealth, religion, art, love—over and over, in one way or another, in fiction or autobiography, Dreiser had defined each of these things as an "illusion." Now, in *An American Tragedy*, he specifically comes upon his final subject, the illusion of the self; for, whatever its origins, consciousness, with all the pathos of aspiration and desire, exists. The "mulch of chemistry" in man that gives him all his other illusions, gives him this, the primary illusion; and the drama of self-definition remains crucial. The last anguish is the yearning for identity, for the illusion that is the fundamental "truth," and Clyde Griffiths, now past all the other empty yearnings that had merely been masks for this deepest yearning, longs for this certainty as he walks down the corridor toward the fatal door at the end. But when, with his last "earthly thought and strength," he replies "good-by all" to the farewells of the condemned men whose turns have not yet come, his voice sounds "so strange and weak, even to himself, so far distant as though it emanated from another being walking alongside of him, and not from himself." What "self" he knows dissolves as now his feet walk "automatically" toward the door that would open to receive him and as quickly close upon "all the earthly life he had ever known" and upon the last illusion.*

As soon as *An American Tragedy* was off the press, people began to ask what kind of tragedy, if any, it was. Clyde Griffiths scarcely seemed to be a tragic hero. He had not fallen from great place. He was not of great scale. Rather than being a man of action, he was acted upon. By what criteria might he be called tragic? Even readers who felt the power of the novel were troubled by the title.

The puzzlement was compounded by the notion that if Dreiser had used this title for his Trilogy (of which only two volumes had then appeared), nobody would have been surprised. Cowperwood, that is, appeared to be every inch the stuff of tragedy. If not of kingly blood, he was, like Tamburlaine, the stuff of which kings are made. His scale was beyond dispute, his power over men, women, and events preternatural. As for his ability to act, he was will incarnate in action. As far as the readers of 1925 were concerned, it seemed that one merely had to wait for the third volume to find the classic conclusion of a tragedy, complete with pity and terror; and even now, with *The Stoic* before us and the dwindling out of the hero with Bright's disease as the conclusion, we may remember that Marlowe's character, too, merely died a natural death, without losing his franchise as a tragic hero.

The comparison of Cowperwood and Clyde is essential for an understanding of what Dreiser is about in *An American Tragedy*; and it is reasonably clear that Dreiser himself was thinking and feeling in these terms. The hard, hypnotic, blazing blue gaze of Cowperwood, before which men quailed and women shivered delightedly, is the central fact of his image, insisted upon again and again. Clyde's eyes, too, are central for his image, and are insisted upon. In the very beginning, even as we are told that Clyde was "as vain and proud as he was poor," and was "one of those interesting individuals who looked upon himself as a thing apart" (as the young Dreiser had sung the refrain to himself, "No common man am I"), we see him studying his assets in a mirror: "a straight, well-cut nose, high white forehead, wavy, glossy black hair, eyes that were black and rather melancholy at times." It is those "deep and rather appealing eyes" that, when a girl cashier in a drugstore notices him, put him in the way of his first good job, in the Green-Davidson hotel. And when the other bellhops take him to his first brothel, the prostitute, trying to overcome his timidity, says, "I like your eyes. You're not like those other fellows. You're more refined, kinda."

Many others, including, of course, Sondra, are to feel the peculiar attraction of his eyes, but they are most obviously important in the stages of the affair with Roberta. There is the moment when she first becomes aware of the "darkness and melancholy and lure of his eyes" and, at the moment of the first kiss, of the "dark, hungry eyes held very close to hers." Then, in the magnificent scene when, after she has refused to let him come to her room and he leaves her standing in the dark street, she, in the "first, flashing, blinding, bleeding stab of love," thinks: "His beautiful face, his beautiful hands. His eyes." At last, on Big Bittern Lake, trying to steel himself to the deed: "And his dark, liquid, nervous eyes, looking anywhere but at her." And in the instant when she becomes aware of his strange expression and makes her fateful movement toward him in the boat: "And in the meantime his eyes—the pupils of the same growing momentarily larger and more lurid. . . ." And the last image we have of Clyde is through McMillan's memory when, after the execution, he wanders the night street: "Clyde's eyes! That look as he sank limply into that terrible chair, his eyes fixed nervously and, as he thought, appealingly and dazedly upon him and the group surrounding him."

The hard, blaze-blue glance of Cowperwood is the index of unrelenting, self-assertive male force. The dark melancholy gaze of Clyde is not an index of force: rather, of weakness, a device of blackmail by which, somehow, his weakness feeds on the kindly or guilty weakness of others so that pity is in the end converted into complicity. In *Dawn* Dreiser says that he himself had given way "to the whining notion that if something were done for me—much—I would amount to a great deal—a whimper which had taken its rise out of my self-exaggerated deprivations. . . . And which of us is not anxious, or at least willing, to have things done for him?" Cowperwood's glance is the mark of naked self-assertion, Clyde's gaze is a confession of the non-self—blank desire, a primal need to "have things done for him."

The self of Clyde does not exist except in terms of desire—at root the desire to create a self worthy of the fulfillment of desire, to conceal the sniveling worthless self. When Clyde sees girls "accompanied by some man in evening suit, dress shirt, high hat, bow tie, white kid gloves and patent leather shoes," he thinks: "To be able to wear such a suit with such ease and air!" And if he did attain such raiment, would he not be "well set upon the path that leads to all the blisses?" And so Dreiser develops, not by a woman but by a man, Clyde or himself, the philosophy of clothes that he had begun in *Sister Carrie*: now at a deeper level, an existential level, a level at which we understand the inwardness of the sad little tale of his embezzlement of $25.00 for the flashy overcoat and of his passion for fame, both as manifestations of the need to create a self, or to conceal the unworthy self.

To sum up, Cowperwood, with his brutal self-sufficiency, can make his way with women, but Clyde is like Dreiser, who could say of himself: "I was too cowardly to make my way with women readily; rather they made their way with me." So we see, for example, that Hortense, Rita, and Sondra "make their way" with Clyde; they have reasons for using him, Hortense for money, Sondra to spite the Griffiths of Lycurgus. Clyde, with his dark, melancholy eyes, merely happens to be handy. Roberta, too, in her own fashion, makes her way with him, as Dreiser quite explicitly puts it, for she has been seized by the "very virus of ambition and unrest that afflicted him."

Her own purposes, however shadowy and unadmitted to herself, are at work, but these purposes are transformed into love, while the purposes of Clyde, in his shadowy inner world of self-concern and self-deception, are not. Since Roberta is in love, and he is not, he can dominate her. But there is another factor involved here. Sondra is in love with Clyde too, and he does not dominate her; rather, with her he remains the passive yearner, the one who must "have things done for him," and it is appropriate that she talks baby talk to him. Underlying the difference between his dominance of

‡ *135* ‡

Roberta and his subservience to Sondra is the difference in social scale. To Sondra, Clyde feels socially inferior, this feeling of inferiority fusing with his other feelings of weakness; but he has sensed that Roberta accepts him as a social superior who stoops to her, who can "do something" for her, and this feeling fuses with his satisfaction in his sexual dominance here achieved for the first time.

So we find, in the instant when Roberta, alarmed by the expression on her lover's face, moves toward him in the boat, this fundamentally significant sentence: "And Clyde, as instantly sensing the profoundness of his own failure, his own cowardice and inadequateness for such an occasion, as instantly yielding to a tide of submerged hate, not only for himself, but for Roberta—her power— or that of life to restrain him in this way." Roberta, the one woman whom he, as a male, has been able to dominate, now seeks to dominate him: she would thwart his desire. And in this instant of her return to the old role all women had had with him, he sensed the "profound-ness" of his own failure—that is, his life-failure, his sexual failure—and the "submerged hate" bursts forth, and poor Roberta pays for all the pent-up and undecipherable hatred and self-hatred Clyde had found in those relationships.

The hate that bursts forth from its secret hiding place does not, it must be emphasized, eventuate in an act of will. Dreiser is explicit: "And yet fearing to act in any way . . ." If the hand holding the camera flies out, the gesture is one of revulsion and self-protection—of flight that somehow comes with an overtone of sexual flight. If Roberta falls into the water and drowns, he is "innocent." And here we are concerned with something different from a mere illustration of unconscious motive, for the episode has a deeper and more ironical implication in which the psychological dimension merges into the metaphysical. Clyde, the blackmailer with the dark, melancholy eyes, Clyde who wanted things done for him, Clyde the Aladdin with the magic lamp—now in this, the great crisis of his life, his deepest wish comes true. The Efrit has served him faithfully, to the end: "For despite your fear, your cowardice, this—this—has been done for you."

His wish is his doom. It is his doom in the deepest sense, for his "innocence" is here the index of his failure to have achieved a self, an identity.*

To return to our question, if Clyde is merely the passive yearner who "wants things done for him," in what sense is his story a tragedy? The first stage toward an answer may be in the adjective "American," which is best explained by a remark, in *A Hoosier Holiday*, about the atmosphere of American cities that, Dreiser says, he has always missed abroad: the "crude, sweet illusion about the importance of things material"—the importance, as he puts it elsewhere in a passage already quoted, of "getting on." Clyde's dream is that "crude, sweet illusion," tragic in that for this mere illusion all values of life, and life itself, will be thrown away.

But behind this illusion is the illusion that in terms

of "getting on" a self may be created, or an unworthy self concealed and redeemed. So here, again, as in the Trilogy, illusion is the key. With Cowperwood the tragic effect lies in the fact that the hero of great scale and force spends himself on illusion—the illusions of will, love, and art. But the hero who seems so self-sufficient, whose "blazing trail . . . did for the hour illuminate the terrors and wonders of individuality," is in the end only, as Dreiser puts it in the epilogue to *The Financier*, the "prince of a world of dreams whose reality was disillusion." So Dreiser, in Clyde Griffiths, turns his attention to another "prince of dreams." What does it matter if Clyde cannot achieve the "soul-dignity," the sense of identity, that Cowperwood could feel even when, in prison, he stared up at the indifferent constellations? What does it matter, for even that sense of "soul-dignity," though it is the illusion that is the only "truth," is but an illusion?

In the story of Clyde, Dreiser is trying to write the root tragedy. It is a tragedy concerned, as tragedy must be, with the nature of destiny, but, as the root tragedy, it seeks the lowest common denominator of tragic effect, an effect grounded in the essential human situation. It is a type of tragedy based on the notion that, on whatever scale, man's lot is always the same. He is the mechanism envisioned by Jacques Loeb, but he is a mechanism with consciousness. His tragedy lies in the doubleness of his nature. He is doomed, as mechanism, to enact a certain role. As a consciousness, he is doomed to seek self-definition in the "terrors and wonders of individuality," the last illusion and the source of final pain.*

Some few human beings seem to avoid the doom,

those who envisage a meaning beyond the natural order of life. For instance, Clyde's mother praying, on the night of his execution, for the soul of her son. In her prayer she affirms: "I know in whom I have believed."

Does she?

In December 1925, *An American Tragedy* was published, in two volumes.* Dreiser, fearing a bad press, had fled New York for Florida, taking Helen with him. There he received his publisher's telegraphed news that the reception was good. Superstitiously, he refused to read reviews, secretly kept in touch with various ladies who were rivals for his favors, quarreled bitterly with Helen, and wrote in his diary, "Wretched days with someone I really don't care to be with." He was about to have another bitter quarrel with Mencken, who reviewed the novel and found it a very mixed bag. It was, he said, "a shapeless and forbidding monster—a heaping cartload of raw materials for a novel with rubbish of all sorts intermixed." If it was, as a work of art, a "colossal botch," he could, nevertheless, add that "as a human document, it is searching and full of solemn dignity." But it didn't really matter what Mencken thought now. With or without Mencken, Dreiser was, at last, a success.

Money poured in, from the novel, the movie rights, and the play (for which, on the opening night, a hired claque yelled "Bravo, Dreiser!"). He set himself up, with Helen, in a luxurious apartment, hired a butler, and had Thursday evenings "at home." He loathed corporations, and played the stock market. He went to Russia as a guest of the government, and found the masses "as Asiatic and dreadful as ever," quarreled with cab drivers, and ended up by writing a trivial and slovenly book about his impressions, in which he plagiarized from Dorothy Thompson. He built an eccentric and expensive house in the country. He continued to pursue, sometimes successfully, all sorts of ladies, tortured Helen, and published *A Gallery of Women*, which may be regarded as a sort of trophy room in print. He dabbled in spiritualism. He published *Dawn*, the first part of his autobiography which had been written some years before, and outraged his sisters by the revelations about their early sexual adventures.

Meanwhile the stock market crash of 1929 came, and Sinclair Lewis (whom not long before Dreiser had slugged in an altercation over the plagiarism from Dorothy Thompson, then Lewis' wife) won the Nobel Prize over Dreiser.

The coming of the Depression meant that Dreiser was more and more involved in social and economic questions, matters on which he had violent and often contradictory opinions and wild prejudices, and at the same time was working on a book intended to be a systematic presentation of his general philosophy. He led a committee to Harlan County, Kentucky, to investigate conditions in the coal fields, and got himself indicted on two counts, criminal syndicalism and adultery. He wrote a disastrously bad book called *Tragic America*. He was flirting with Communism, and when, in 1932, he tried to join the Party and was turned down (quite logically) by Earl Browder, he was outraged. He was deep in causes, committees, and campaigns, defending Tom Mooney, who was in jail in California, and taking up Technocracy. He was a founder, with George Jean Nathan, Ernest Boyd, Eugene O'Neill, and James Branch Cabell, of a new high-brow magazine, the *American Spectator*. He loathed the English even more than he loathed corporations, and had kind words for Nazism. He had lunch with President Roosevelt on the subject of relief for Spain, now in the midst of the Franco revolution. When, in 1939, the Berlin-Moscow Pact was signed, Dreiser praised Hitler's wisdom and goodness. When war began and Roosevelt favored the allies, he wrote: "I begin to suspect that Hitler is correct. The president may be part Jewish." Dreiser also began to cherish the notion that the firm currently suffering as his publishers, Simon and Schuster, were in a Jewish plot to suppress his works. He joined the American Peace Mobilization and made a violently anti-English speech in Washington to an outdoor mass rally. When, after difficulties, he succeeded in getting a printer for his rabid and incoherent book *America Is Worth Saving* (a title changed at the last minute from *Is America Worth Saving?*), he sent an autographed copy to Joseph Stalin. At the news of Hitler's attack on Russia, Dreiser simply retreated to his bed.

Dreiser's health was not good, and clearly his mind was failing. He felt defeated and forgotten. But he managed to do some work on his fiction, for he was still nursing the old Quaker novel, *The Bulwark,* and the last item of the Trilogy, *The Stoic.* He wrote a pietistic essay called "My Creator," which indicated the drift his fiction was taking. *The Bulwark*, which, in fact, had started out years ago as an attack on religion, was becoming a story of Job in modern dress, and Dreiser even attended church (Congregational, not Catholic) and took communion. Shortly afterward, however, he applied again for membership in the Communist Party (in a letter appropriate for publication, written for him by Party-trained hands expert with the language of propaganda), and was accepted. Even with ill health, he still found energy for his sexual intrigues, including (after he had again fled to California) a ten-day honeymoon in a Los Angeles hotel with an admirer whom he had never seen but whom he had lured west from Detroit. But on June 13, 1944, he married Helen.

It was the last phase. *The Bulwark* finished and turned over to one of the faithful lady editors, Dreiser resumed work on *The Stoic*, dictating to Helen. His strength was failing fast. On December 27, 1945, in accordance with suggestions from James Farrell, who had read the manuscript for him, Dreiser revised the penultimate chapter of the Trilogy. Before dawn, he suffered an attack, and was put in an oxygen mask. He died late in the afternoon of December 28. A Congregational minister had prayed at the bedside. Just before he died he asked Helen, now at long last his wife, to kiss him.

Dreiser was buried in Forest Lawn Cemetery, in Los Angeles, among the movie moguls and movie stars and their hangers-on, for which final glory he had, no doubt, yearned. At the funeral ceremony, the Congregational minister who had prayed by the bedside spoke, then John Howard Lawson, a successful movie writer who had shepherded Dreiser into the Communist Party. By way of conclusion, Charlie Chaplin read Dreiser's poem "The Road I Came," the last lines of which are:

> Oh, what is this
> That knows the road I came?

In 1951, Helen published *My Life with Dreiser*, with the dedication:

> To the unknown women in the life of Theodore Dreiser, who devoted themselves unselfishly to the beauty of his intellect and its artistic unfoldment.

NOTES

page 11

In answer to a request for information about the exact address at which Dreiser was born, Richard W. Dowell (editor of the *Dreiser Newsletter*, Indiana State University, Terre Haute) writes:

> Dreiser's birthplace in Terre Haute has never been conclusively identified, but enough is known to allow some guesses. This much I have been able to determine:
>
> When Dreiser was conceived, the family was living in Sullivan, Indiana, where his father was either leasing or managing a woolen mill owned by Terre Haute millionaire Chauncey Rose. The mill was apparently damaged sometime early in 1871, for Rose sold the property at a considerable loss in February. John Paul Dreiser then sold his Sullivan home in March and the remainder of his Sullivan property the following month. Thus, the family probably returned to Terre Haute in the early spring of 1871. The above is based on Sullivan real estate records.
>
> The Dreisers do not appear in the 1871 Terre Haute city directory, but the real estate records show that the father purchased a home at 203 South 12th Street for $1,200 on September 11, 1871, the day after Theodore was baptized at St. Benedict's Catholic Church in Terre Haute. The family apparently lived at this address until May, 1878, when John Paul Dreiser sold the property for $1,400. This permanent address for almost seven years suggests that the standard picture of the poverty-driven Dreisers being harried from hovel to hovel is much exaggerated. Most of the addresses Dreiser gives in his various references to Terre Haute do not appear in the city directory.
>
> But back to the birthplace. The facts would seem to indicate that Dreiser was born in a rented house the Dreisers occupied briefly after they returned from Sullivan. Dreiser has suggested such locations as 9th Street (*Dawn*, p. 7) and the corner of 9th and Chestnut (*A Hoosier Holiday*, p. 402). A local historian, the late A. R. Markle, has decided that the address was 525 South 9th, an address that no longer exists

in Terre Haute. Markle came to this conclusion through correspondence with Dreiser's sister Mame, who was eighty at the time. She remembered the names of neighbors whom Markle was able to track down in the city directory. Then, he took pictures of houses in what seemed to be the logical area and sent them to Mame for identification. She selected one as Theodore's birthplace. Mame was ten at the time of Dreiser's birth. Few people, I might add, have faith in Markle's process and conclusion, but to date no one has come up with a more convincing theory.

page 13

On the basis of this strange and troubling passage, it is easy to believe that the son may have learned more than pity. It is easy, for instance, to believe that Sarah Dreiser's words would carry the message that her wearing of such shoes was all the fault of John Paul Dreiser—the man whom the son was later to hope that she had betrayed. So Sarah's words may really be a way of demanding not only sympathy, but protection—and, even, vengeance. It may be objected that the event may never have occurred, that Dreiser dreamed it up; in that case, the imagined episode would be more deeply significant than the real could have been.

page 18

To Mencken, who had edited Nietzsche, Dreiser was later to say that he regarded his friend's hero as nothing more than "Schopenhauer confused and warmed over." But in the ordinary man-in-the-street way, Dreiser, with his adoration of the superman, was the perfect Nietzschean.

page 25

See Kenneth S. Lynn: *The Dream of Success*, Boston, 1935, p. 24.

page 27

When Drouet gives Carrie her first pretty clothes, Dreiser presents a little scene of remarkable psychological insight. Admiring herself, Carrie catches "her little red lip with her teeth" and feels "her first thrill of power." Here the biting of her own lip, with its charge of narcissistic sexuality, is fused with the "thrill of power."

page 28

In this connection, to look ahead, it was after *An American Tragedy*, when Dreiser had at last achieved fame and wealth as a writer and was living in an elegant apartment, employing a butler, entertaining lavishly, and playing the stock market, that he began to rail at the money-madness of the age, the tyranny of great corporations, and the nervous fluidity of American life. Dreiser, with all his memories of the old pinch of poverty, and with his aspirations to "social supremacy" that could be gratified only in a democratic plutocracy, began, in a final and contradictory irony, to regret the dissolution of the hierarchical society of the Middle Ages—a strange manifestation of his superstitious sense of guilt. But no stranger than the impulse that drew him to admire John Burroughs and to edit Thoreau.

page 29

As one of the various subtle structural "ties" or "cross references" in the novel, we find that when Carrie is left alone, after Drouet has made his suggestion that she act in the play being put on by his lodge, she sits in a rocking chair and indulges, for the first time, the flood of daydreams of theatrical glory—the anticipation of glory, and the discovery of the blankness of glory, both belong in the rocking chair. This scene affords another cross reference, here to another novel, *The Titan*, with the episode of Stephanie the actress. As we shall see later, the artist (specifically actress) lives outside ordinary sanctions and fidelities, for the obligation is to the "illusion" of art (specifically to the role, with the role existing out of time); so it is only the artist (Stephanie the actress and Berenice the painter) who can overcome, however briefly, the powerful Cowperwood, Dreiser's version of a Robber Baron. The parallel here is that Carrie's discovery of her "artistic nature" leads, first, to the betrayal of Drouet, and second, to her abandonment of Hurstwood.

page 52

This touch, one of the few moments of depth in the whole book, may be taken as a forerunner of the scene in *An American*

Tragedy, when Clyde, in his death cell, cannot determine the nature of his guilt or the significance of his religious conversion. In quite another connection, one may surmise that, however remotely, this scene lies behind the death of Catherine in *A Farewell to Arms*: both birth scenes are quite specifically based on the contrast between the irrational "trap" of nature on one side, and human dreams and passions on the other, and both scenes present the formal initiation of the hero into his fate. Frederick Henry must recognize himself as the "man alone," and Eugene Witla must recognize his own role in life. Further, Thomas Wolfe's *Of Time and the River* is in many ways similar to *The "Genius,"* even in the name of the hero.

page 53

It would seem that Dreiser switches Witla from journalist to artist as a way of emphasizing this point of the locus of "reality," the journalist, by definition, being tied to fact.

page 55

The date of the publication of the book is misleading. In March 1881, Lloyd had published, in the *Atlantic Monthly*, then under the editorship of William Dean Howells, an unprecedented article entitled "The Story of a Great Monopoly," a shocking exposé of the methods by which Standard Oil had seized its power that became the germ of the book of thirteen years later. Howells' social convictions and editorial acumen were working in harmony; that issue of the *Atlantic* promptly ran through seven printings.

page 59

When in 1927 Dreiser visited Russia, he used the same argument in defending American capitalism against a Soviet factory manager—as he reports in *Dreiser Looks at Russia*.

page 60

Elsewhere in his book Hofstadter points out that Beard, as a young man, just after the panic of 1893, visited Chicago, to see the booming pretensions and the squalor and ugliness.

page 61

Holmes, of course, had a logicality and self-consistency that neither Beard nor Dreiser could boast. Even in the dissent of Vegelahn v. Guntner, Holmes based his argument on the idea of the "eternal conflict out of which life is made up," and of which economic competition happens to be the immediate example to point, and on the idea that life is "experiment" rather than on the abstract social idealism that liberals sometimes attributed to him. Strangely enough, Holmes, in his intellectual consistency, would be closer, ultimately, to Dreiser than to the intellectuals like Beard. For Holmes, in his philosophy, was willing to submit his intellectuality to the "experiment" of life— which was precisely what Dreiser's fiction represents; the act of submitting his ideas, and himself, to the paradoxicality and disintegrative fluidity of experience: he could "be" both Carrie and Jennie, Cowperwood and Clyde Griffiths. But more of this later.

page 65

There are a number of provocative similarities between Mark Twain and Dreiser, in addition to their ambivalence about success and "getting somewhere." Each was a "mother's child," to use Dreiser's phrase about himself, and each hated his father. Both wanted to have things "done for them." For instance, Mark Twain played such a role to the hilt with "Mother Fairbanks," a somewhat older lady whom he adopted as social and literary mentor, and cunningly used it as a tactic in courting the girl he married, and in courting her family. Here even the "Aladdinish dream" comes in, for after the marriage to Olivia Langdon, with the unexpected wedding present from his father-in-law of a mansion and an appropriate bank account, and in the first bliss of matrimony, Mark Twain could refer to himself as "Little Sammy in Fairyland." Like Dreiser, too, Mark Twain came to regard man as "merely a machine . . . moved wholly by outside influences." And in the end, he too saw all as illusion, as in the unfinished story called "The Great Dark" and in a letter to Sue Crane, his sister-in-law:

> I dreamed that I was born and grew up and was a pilot on
> the Mississippi and a miner and a journalist in Nevada and
> a pilgrim in the *Quaker City* [the steamer on which he was
> one of the "innocents abroad"], and had a wife and children

and went to live in a villa at Florence—and this dream
goes on and on and sometimes seems so real that I almost
believe it is real. But there is no way to tell, for if one
applied tests they would be part of the dream, too, and so
would simply aid the deceit. I wish I knew whether it is a
a dream or real.

page 68

This perversion lies, presumably, in the fact that Cowperwood
does not finally enjoy sex except as it involves the elements of
resistance, competition, and conquest—the key to his own
nature. The conquest of Lillian Semple promises to be especially
sweet. The "pale, uncertain, lymphatic body" had not, he intuits,
ever been aroused—a body not readily aroused to begin with,
and certainly not aroused by Mr. Semple, the shoe merchant.
Let us look more closely at the phrase "love him vigorously." It
seems a strange and awkward one—until we take the word
"love" in its most literal sense, and then the word "vigorously"
comes alive in the sudden, unexpected energy and struggle of
that "lymphatic body" stabbed for the first time to sexual frenzy
and delight. And in thus conquering that body's inner resistance,
the new lover, forcing that body to compare this moment with
previous tepidities and torpor, makes Lillian thus connive in the
"killing" of the old lover. The locution "to love vigorously"
appears also in *Sister Carrie*, Chapter 9, in contrasting Hurstwood's present indifference to his wife with his attitude in the
early days of marriage: "As long as she loves him vigorously . . ."

page 74 (1)

In the ordinary historical novel, literal historical figures usually
become, for all practical purposes, part of the décor.

page 74 (2)

Sister Carrie and *Jennie Gerhardt* are, in fact, retellings of the
tale of the ruined maid, the subject dear to balladry and melo-
drama. We may remember that *Tess of the D'Urbervilles* is
another example of folk material, like Dreiser's novels a tale of the
ruined maid, a tale that had been told over and over in Victorian
England in little tuppenny paperbacks to be read by young
governesses and the more literate female domestics who were

the traditional prey of the full-blooded squire. Nor should we forget that some of Hardy's finest poetry is also rooted in folk-consciousness.

An American Tragedy, too, has its roots in folk tradition, and its inspiration is not far from that of the old tear-jerker, "Oh, Where Is My Wandering Boy Tonight?" or that of Paul Dresser's composition "The Path That Leads the Other Way," or even his "On the Banks Of the Wabash, Far Away," for which Theodore wrote the first stanza:

> Round my Indiana homestead waves the cornfield,
> In the distance loom the woodlands clear and cool.
> Often times my thoughts revert to scenes of childhood,
> Where I first received my lessons, nature's school.
> But one thing there is missing in the picture,
> Without her face it seems so incomplete.
> I long to see my mother in the doorway,
> As she stood there years ago, her boy to greet!

Theodore Dreiser and Paul Dresser were cut off the same bolt of goods—the only difference being that one was a genius. Moers has an excellent account of the folk elements in both Paul and Theodore. But Paul's songs were also a late development of the "Fireside School" of American poetry. In the first third of the nineteenth century, under the poetic consulship of Mrs. Sarah Josepha Hale and Mrs. Lydia Sigourney (the "Sweet Singer of Hartford"), the "home" was the focus of all emotion. Infant innocence and family solidarity were important subjects, but the mother was the center of all. The character who speaks in Mrs. Sigourney's poem "Power of Maternal Piety" declares that

> In foreign lands I travelled wide,
> My pulse was beating high,
> Vice spread her meshes at my side,
> And pleasure lured my eye.

But he heard, as "from the lowly sod," his mother's voice admonishing him:

> "My son—my only one—beware!
> Nor sin against they God."

Mrs. Hale, who often seems to be doubling for Mrs. Sigourney, warns a son in "The Light of Home":

> My boy, thou wilt dream the world is fair,
> And thy spirit will sigh to roam;

> And thou must go: but never when there,
> Forget the light of home.

Against the expansion of the new country and the centrifugal pull of the West and of the sea, there was "home"—the glowing fireside with the window shut against the old fear of the forest and the new challenge of destiny. Paul Dresser, runaway, wanderer, *bon vivant*, and whore-master, ironically made the last desperate effort to nail the window shut for good. He could afford to; he was already outside.

page 77

Fuller continued to write well into the twentieth century; his last novel was published posthumously in 1930.

page 78

At the end of *The Titan*, in the relation with Berenice, when Cowperwood is, for a moment, victimized by illusion, it might be said that here we do have a sense of process in time; but this impression that Cowperwood has come to a "truth" is quickly repudiated, in the epilogue of the novel. The only character in the Trilogy who really "grows old" is Aileen. She is not treated as a specimen, even though, as a mate for the superman, Dreiser may have originally regarded her as one; she lives as a creature in time, suffering fundamental changes. As a matter of fact, whatever Dreiser's intentions, she serves as an index of Cowperwood's changelessness. As for Berenice, her conversion is purely arbitrary, dictated by thematic considerations. What we have is not a sense of change in time so much as intensification in time, an elaboration of dialectic.

page 79

Yerkes himself seems to have had something of this trait. When he burst in on a group of Chicago financiers gathered at the house of Philip D. Armour to plot his ruin, he could remark, "I never before saw so many straw hats at a funeral." Some other Robber Barons also had the redeeming salt of wit.

page 81

In *Dawn*, which belongs to the same general period as the Trilogy, Dreiser writes: "Life's greatest lures are a compound of illusion—phantasms, mirages, *ignes fatui*, I fear—I do not know —but like the mystery which binds people to religious beliefs, so was I bound. I have also sometimes wondered whether the power of nature to delude us is ever broken, even in the days when we are but thin and decayed fibre of former physical strength. If imagination endures, unquestionably the power of nature to charm and betray is there." Dreiser is here referring (Chapter 28) to his falling in love during the period at the University—with a girl whom he scarcely knew and never talked to—one of the "five cases" in which he was laid hold of "as by an iron force." But if here he refers to the illusion of love, what he says applies to all illusions. For instance, later in *Dawn*, in connection with his period as a bill collector for a company selling gaudy gimcrack rugs, clocks, and lamps to the poor, he speaks of art as illusion (though without using the word); and then comes to wealth: "For what is hoarding of wealth, after all, but illusion?" And at the end of *Dawn*, he asks: "What, cooking, eating, coition, job-holding, growing, aging, losing, winning, in so changeful and passing a scene as this, important? Bunk! It is some form of titillating illusion with about as much import to the superior forces that bring it all about as the functions and gyrations of a fly. No more. And maybe less."

page 82

Stephanie is modeled, in part at least, on Kirah Markham, whom Dreiser met in 1912 when she was twenty and he was in Chicago doing research for *The Titan*. She, like Stephanie, had a Jewish father, was a painter and an actress in the Little Theater of Chicago, a group that receives Dreiser's attention in this novel. She, like Stephanie, became the mistress of the "superman," but did not give a model for Stephanie's infidelities.

page 83

See note for p. 29.

page 85

Dreiser, though seeing man caught in the great machine of nature, does allow him the dignity of the "terror and wonder of individuality." A more devoted and systematic naturalist, like Henry Adams, would scarcely, however, allow such dignity. In his *His-*

tory of the United States in the Administrations of Jefferson and Madison, Adams, for instance, describes those two statesmen who tried to create a true democracy, as nothing more than puppets of history, or as "mere grasshoppers kicking and gesticulating" while borne away down the stream of time into darkness. For all his "chemisms," Dreiser is not quite ready to say, with Margoth, the brutal geologist in Melville's *Clarel*, that "All is Chymistry."

page 90

The litigation came to nothing, the case being, in the end, thrown out on a technicality: no copy had been actually sold in violation of the injunction. The case did, however, prepare the way for the liberal decisions of the next decade.

page 92

During this period there is a small episode that may be of significance. To an unknown young man who had sent letters to newspapers in defense of *The "Genius,"* Dreiser, in thanking him, wrote: "And I give you one kindly piece of advice. Never bother to know me, personally. Remain illusioned, if you can."

page 95

The fact that Dreiser was of German blood had been drawn into the attacks on *The "Genius."*

page 97

In what we possess of *The Rake*, the young Ansley Bellinger bears little resemblance in social class, education, or the events of his career to Clyde Griffiths; but though we do not know how it was to be worked out, we do have evidence that the tension between the world of privilege and that of poverty was to be somehow central to the conception. The manuscript begins with the sentence: "In those days the city of New York and more especially the heart of the central island—Manhattan—was the centre of a kind of pagan glory that fairly recalled the heroic splendors of Rome." This world of "hard materialisms," Dreiser says, was a "strange fruition of the vine of Democracy"—a "seething realm of show, of sex of love, as indeed, and also, of emulation and of despair" on the part of the outsiders "envying the joy of those who had all."

Presumably, the outsider of *The Rake* was not to be poor. Young Bellinger's father had accumulated a "comfortable fortune," but everything is relative, and the son was, we are told, merely on "the hem of established privilege," one of those "striving to keep up the social pretense." Young Bellinger does, however, resemble Clyde in having "shabby affairs" with girls of the lower class, and, like Clyde, is a dreamer, being described as having the "imagination to invest the female form with a kind of glory which really was not there." Actually, the description of Bellinger resembles, even in verbal parallels, Witla of *The "Genius"* more than Clyde, but there seems to be no other evidence to suggest that *The Rake* is an early form of that work, as some critics have held. In fact, there are complex interrelations among Dreiser's individual works, and Dreiser was often fumbling, in one thing, toward what might be the central vision of another. For instance, in *Sister Carrie* there are elements much more closely related to *An American Tragedy* than is anything in *The Rake*, and this leads to the idea that a manuscript fragment entitled "Her Boy" is closer than either to the story of Clyde. The "Boy"—Eddie—is of a very poor family, dislikes his father (who, unlike Asa Griffiths or John Paul Dreiser, is an idle, drunken brute—but the mere fact of the dislike may be significant), has a "very dear memory of one of the streets near his mother's house," and drifts into bad company, vice, and crime. But he is, in a sense, guiltless. "It was not that they [the bad boys] were so darkly dishonest as that the chemism which makes for beauty and the instinct for pleasure which fires all youth was operating in them." Eddie himself is more precisely delineated: ". . . in the poorly combined substances of his chemistry, there were some registrations of beauty and possible phases of happiness—the beauty of girls, for one thing, the fine homes with their flowers and walks to be seen in other parts of the city—windows full of clothing, and musical instruments and interesting things, generally—things he had never known and was destined never to know in any satisfying and comforting way." His is an "errant mind, subject to dreams, vanities, illusions." And in the file called the "Straight Away"—the name given by Dreiser to a group of items presumably having some relation to *An American Tragedy*—"Her Boy" is followed by a sketch of Sarah Schänäb.

page 106 (1)

Or was she only a dream, or not even a dream but a false recollection, a "screen memory" that so vividly summed up desires and fantasies that he took it for a fact?

page 106 (2)

In the 1930's, when Dreiser was visiting San Francisco, he was interviewed by Raymond Dannenbaum [the writer Raymond Dane], editor of the *Jewish Journal*, who reported, in conversation with the present author, that Dreiser was concerned to convince him that he had never suffered from impotence, but that if people got that idea it was sometimes a convenience.

page 107

The whole scene and atmosphere of the laundry that seems an "Adamless paradise where houri were to be had just for the asking," is the model for the room in the factory at Lycurgus where the yearning Clyde prowls among the forbidden girls.

page 109

Notice how in this passage the images combine paradoxically the notions of power and freedom (the petrel) with innocent victimization and innocence (seaweed). The longed-for condition is to be able to enjoy the power and freedom without guilt. Notice, too, how the idea of the "subterranean tides" appears again in the scene of Roberta's murder. Here, Clyde, growing suddenly aware of his "failure," yields to "a tide of submerged hate." But to turn to the matter of style, how can the sea have "subterranean tides"?

page 118

It may be objected that the only language of fiction is words, and in the strict sense this is true. The verbal language does offer us—evoke for us—the sequence of scenes that constitute the action, and it may offer commentary and interpretation as well. But we must always realize that the commentary and interpretation never give us the full meaning, it is only marginal and indicative; the full meaning is embodied in the action. To be satisfied with a fiction, we demand this sense of meaning embodied in action, meaning of a depth and resonance far greater than the verbal language can ever literally declare. Insofar as this is true, the "procession" of events is a language—what psychologists call the "primary" language, the massive and condensed forms in which desire, hate, and fear express themselves, in the primitive dark of our being. The grammar of the primary language of imagery is enormously complex. In this language is the deep locus of what we call the emotional composition of a work, and of the fundamental rhythmic structure; but the grammar of this language refers, too, to the most profound philosophical dialect in a work—but the dialectic as "lived out," not argued out. By the verbal language, the product of ages of culture, the writer evokes the primary language; and a story or poem represents, then, in its very nature a deep tension and interaction of the regressive and the sophisticated, with all the dimensions of general human history and of personal history echoed in that fact. It may be thought that the tension and interaction of the verbal and the primary languages is one of the fundamental factors in determining the form of a literary work. To begin with, we may think of the varying degrees (and kinds) of emphasis writers may place on the verbal language as such; on one hand, for example, Henry James, Proust, Eudora Welty, and on the other, Defoe, Swift, John O'Hara. Or we may think of the varying degrees of reliance on commentary and interpretation we find in the verbal language. By the same token, we may think of the varying degrees (and kinds) of complexity in primary language. The "ratio" between the verbal and the primary languages becomes, then, a control of fictional form.

page 127 (1)

In *A Hoosier Holiday*, when Dreiser returns to Terre Haute and puts up at the hotel where his mother had once been a scrubwoman, he describes how the "best" hotel in a town was the focus of dreams. "For here, once upon a time, my brother Rome, at that time a seeking boy like any of those we now saw pouring up and down this well lighted street—(up and down, up and down, day after day, like those poor moths we see about the lamp)—was in the habit of coming, and . . . in his best suit of clothes and his best shoes, a toothpick in his mouth, standing in or near the doorway of the hotel, to give the impression that he had just dined there." But the hotel was also the focus

of the dreams of the well-to-do who came there to exhibit themselves and prove their success: "The flare of the cloth of their
suits! The blaze of their skins and eyes! The hardy, animal
implication of their eyes!"

page 127 (2)

The Aladdin theme appears, in fact, as early as *Sister Carrie*,
in Chapter 16, entitled "A Witless Aladdin: The Gate to the
World," in which Drouet, almost by accident, arranges for
Carrie's first stage appearance; and the relation of the illusion
of the stage—the dream—and the Aladdin theme reaches to the
center of Dreiser's inspiration.

William L. Phillips, in "The Imagery of Dreiser's Novels" (*Publication of the Modern Language Association*, December, 1963),
points out more specifically that the basic image of *An American
Tragedy* is one of dream, and that in this novel Dreiser abandons
the imagery of nature, such as that of the lobster and the squid,
or that of climate (or morality) in *The Financier,* for this imagery
of the inward and indeterminate, of subjectivity. Ellen Moers, in
The Two Dreisers, works out a detailed parallel between the
Aladdin story and that of Clyde in connection with Clyde's flight
from reality.

page 129

I have said "secularized society" because the only persons who
offer a notion of the self that Dreiser can set against the
machine of the world are Clyde's mother and the Reverend
McMillan. This is not to say that Dreiser is offering a doctrinal
solution, but it is to say that only in the image drawn from
religion does he, ironically enough, with all the ambivalences,
find an image of the responsible self, and an image of the possibility of meaningfulness in the hymn that Clyde's family lifts
up, as evening crowds bustle by, "against the vast skepticism
and apathy of life."

A number of critics, in fact, have noted, in spite of Dreiser's
notion of life as a great, blind, amoral process, that his work
in general is shot through with a tortured moral sensibility.
This paradox should not (though it often does) cause surprise,
for paradox, opposition, and contradiction are central to
Dreiser's nature and to his work. We can, indeed, think of the
idea of good and evil as one of the key illusions of the Dreiserian

drama. It, like will, love, "art-dreams," and the self, is set against the blankness of the constellations, the face, "gross and cruel and mechanical," of modern society, and the pitiless chemism of the human constitution, and as such an illusion, it is pervasive in Dreiser's fiction with, generally, the same status as that of the other illusions. But we may remind ourselves that in one instance the idea of good and evil does seem to receive a privileged status. *Jennie Gerhardt* celebrates the triumphant peace of goodness that survives the defeats and pains of the secular world, and there is no hint here that Jennie's values are illusory, and Jennie, unlike Dreiser's other heroes and heroines, does not need our pity. *Jennie Gerhardt* is, of course, an early book, but already, in *Sister Carrie*, Dreiser had clearly foreshadowed the world of amoral forces that he was to describe explicitly in the Trilogy, *The "Genius,"* and *An American Tragedy*, and had foreshadowed, with the rocking chair and the copy of *Père Goriot*, the doctrine of illusion.

In the end, Dreiser—even as he was finishing the last volume of the Trilogy—could not rest content with the doctrine of illusion. Old John Paul Dreiser had his innings at last, for the son, as life closed in on him, took refuge in a confused religiosity. Paradoxically enough, he took refuge, too, in the Communist Party. His nerve had failed.

page 130

Loeb appears as Max Gottlieb in *Arrowsmith*, by Sinclair Lewis.

page 131

The scene of the execution receives much of its force from a parabolic dimension, recessive though inevitable—a dimension that would be appreciated by the author of *Waiting for Godot* and *Endgame*.

page 137

On several occasions I have referred to Clyde's "innocence," and what is at stake here lies at the very center of *An American Tragedy*. Of those critics who would stress Clyde's innocence the most recent is Richard Lehan, for whom Clyde is "really innocent" and "legally innocent"—and is, in fact, the "innocent dreamer caught in a web of antithetical forces." As a corollary to this idea, Lehan specifically contradicts Van Wyck Brooks' notion that Dreiser portrayed in Reverend McMillan "the Protestant minister as he ought to be," and Lionel Trilling's similarly favorable interpretation.

Here Lehan refers to the scene in which McMillan goes with Clyde's mother to make a final appeal to the Governor of New York, and the Governor, a decent man, asks him if he, as Clyde's spiritual adviser, knows "of any material fact not introduced at the trial which would in any way tend to invalidate or weaken any phase of the testimony offered at the trial." Lehan says: "Although Clyde is legally innocent, McMillan believes that he is guilty before God and, as a result, fails to give the Governor the facts that could save Clyde's life." Let us note that Lehan insists on a sharp distinction between being guilty before God and being guilty before the law, with the clear statement that, though McMillan knew facts that would exculpate Clyde before the law, he deliberately withheld them because he regarded him as guilty before God. This reading simply contradicts the plain statement in the novel: "Had he [McMillan] not decided, after due meditation as to Clyde's confession [to him], that he was guilty before God *and the law* [italics mine]?" And the next sentence runs: "And could he now—for mercy's sake—and in the face of his deepest spiritual conviction, alter his report of his conviction?" In other words, Lehan to the mysterious contrary, there are no "facts" which, if offered to the Governor, "could save Clyde's life."

We are, therefore, thrown back on McMillan's conviction —or rather, on the question of the reasonableness of his conviction—that Clyde is guilty before *both* God and the law. We know the pattern of events as Dreiser states them in the scene of the murder: (1) aware of his "failure," Clyde yields "to a tide of submerged hate, not only for himself, but Roberta"; (2) "fearing to act," Clyde would now be willing only to say that he would never marry Roberta, but not able to say that, even, he is left "angry and confused and glowering"; (3) he flings out at her with no "intention to do other than free himself," but with the camera "unconsciously held tight"; (4) "stirred by her sharp scream," he rises "half to assist or recapture her and half to apologize for the unintended blow"; (5) once the boat has capsized and Roberta is drowning, he hears the voice of the Efrit: "An accident—an accident—an unintentional blow on your part is now saving you the labor of what you sought, and yet did not have the courage to do! . . . Rest but a moment—a fraction of a minute"; (6) "swimming heavily, gloomily and darkly to shore," he thanks God he had not "really" killed her. "And yet . . . had he?" The episode ends with the unresolvable oscillation in his mind between guilt and innocence: "And yet—and yet—"

The account given in Clyde's confession to McMillan substantially follows Dreiser's own, but it is worth rehearsing the key points involved in the episode: (1) Clyde admits that the main contention of the defense, that he had had a change of heart, was a "lie"; (2) he still finds in the event "much that was evasive and even insoluble" and is unable "to demonstrate to himself even—either his guilt or his lack of guilt"; (3) he admits "anger" in the blow, even if the blow was unconscious; (4) when McMillan asks if he had "really" intended to catch Roberta, after the blow while she teetered in the boat, Clyde says: "I don't know. At the moment I guess I did. Anyhow I felt sorry, I think"; (5) he admits that he had deliberately refrained from going to assist Roberta in the water, and that, at the moment, he had had thoughts of "Miss X"; (6) McMillan says to Clyde, "In your heart was murder then," and Clyde replies, "I have thought since it must have been that way"; (7) later, when McMillan is privately wrestling with the ambiguities of the situation, we find the summarizing lines: "McMillan was against capital punishment . . . But none-the-less felt himself compelled to acknowledge, Clyde was far from innocent. Think as he would —and however much spiritually he desired to absolve him, was he not actually guilty?"

McMillan is clearly not intended as a bigot who would execute a man he did not believe to be legally guilty. This is explicit, and the fact that McMillan does not believe in capital punishment underscores the fact, and was no doubt intended to guard against exactly the kind of misreading indulged in by Lehan. Lehan is, of course, right in remarking that the episode—and, indeed, the whole novel—is massively shot through with ironies and paradoxes, but in insisting that Clyde is "really innocent" and that McMillan is a treacherous bigot, he would settle for a crude, obvious and mechanical irony and miss the deep, fundamental, and all-penetrating irony of the ambiguity of identity and responsibility.

Furthermore, the existence of this irony would not, it must be emphasized, indicate that Dreiser would have Clyde get off. If Clyde is a pitiable creature, the victim of a doom, all men, and society itself, are, by the same token, merely enacting—

pitiably, to be sure—a doom. A little after *An American Tragedy*, Dreiser was to say: "Life is, as I see it, an organized process about which we can do nothing in the final analysis"; this view was one pole of Dreiser's thought and fiction, or to change the metaphor, the backdrop against which the human drama, with all its tangled questions of moral value, is enacted. And to return to the question of Clyde's innocence, we must remember that, even if Dreiser, watching Clyde in the stage version of his novel, wept and murmured "Poor boy, poor boy," he was capable of refusing support to the League for the Abolition of Capital Punishment.

The versions of *An American Tragedy*, from the first in Dreiser's hand to the typed setting copy in which Dreiser made cuts and wrote in revisions, bear on the matter of McMillan's role. In the setting copy a very important section (different from the early version but substantially the same) is cut. Here McMillan, under constant pressure to make public Clyde's confession to him, finally issues a written statement in which, though refusing to violate the seal of confession, he says: "I now wish to say that in my judgment and *under the law as it stands*, and apart from wisdom and charity which I consider to have been violated, *no legal mistake was made* [italics mine]." To this Belknap and Jephson offer a public rejoinder that is summed up in the words: "Not until we see a confession in Clyde Griffiths' hand writing will we believe that he even confessed to anyone."

Immediately following this in the novel is a newspaper headline, of "three years later":

CLYDE GRIFFITHS SPIRITUAL
ADVISOR A SUICIDE
THE REVEREND DUNCAN MCMILLAN OF SYRACUSE
LEAPS TO DEATH
FROM HOSPITAL WINDOW

The news report runs: McMillan "was seized with melancholia" and sought recovery in travel, but "in the past year he was given to venting scruples in regard to his original decision as to Griffiths' *complete guilt* [italics mine]—though in what way he had erred, he repeatedly stated that as yet he was not ready to say—merely that he was troubled." The passage ends with the statement that no note of explanation had been left.

At first glance this section in the setting copy, cut at the last minute, might be taken to support Lehan's notion (though he makes no reference in this connection to Dreiser's earlier versions), but let us look more closely at the italicized matter, remembering, too, the important fact that Lehan's argument is directed only to McMillan's conduct in the interview with the Governor. Here, in the public statement made some time after that event, McMillan simply repeats his previous belief that Clyde was guilty "under the law as it stands"—even though for McMillan, who is opposed on principle to capital punishment, the law violated wisdom and charity. The Governor has asked McMillan a question about Clyde's situation under the law: if McMillan speaks to that question he must violate "wisdom and charity," and if he speaks in accordance with "wisdom and charity," he must lie. What most obviously Dreiser has done in this deleted material is to emphasize dramatically the dilemma in which McMillan is caught. Let us observe, too, that McMillan goes to his death with the dilemma unresolved. He does not decide that Clyde was innocent and then commit suicide in an anguish of remorse. The point is that he is concerned with the question of "complete guilt" (not merely legal guilt), and it is the unresolvableness of this question that he cannot endure—for it is not an abstract issue but one in which he must deeply live. He is a man committed to absolutes but doomed to live in a world of complex definitions and shadowy ambiguities.

But Dreiser is trying to do something more fundamental than merely to dramatize McMillan's personal entrapment in a dilemma. McMillan's personal dilemma merely illustrates the basic issue of the novel, the question of the nature of guilt—a question that bleeds outward from the question of personal and immediate guilt (which Clyde in the death house confronts, "the troubling question in his own mind as to his real guilt—the amount of it") to the social, physiological, psychological, and metaphysical dimensions.

If this extension of the story of McMillan dramatizes this issue, why, we might ask, should Dreiser have cut it? Possibly because it *does* dramatize the issue and dramatize it in too limited and schematic a fashion. In the final form of the novel we do see McMillan's anguish, but very briefly, with the material of the setting copy much reduced, ending:

> Had he done right? Had his decision before Governor Waltham been truly sound, fair or merciful? Should he have said to him—that perhaps—perhaps—there had been

those other influences playing upon him? . . . Was he never to have mental peace again, perhaps?

"I know my Redeemer liveth and that He will keep him against that day."

With this assertion of his own faith (really a way of admitting that the question is otherwise unresolvable) McMillan goes, as soon as his courage permits, to join Clyde's mother, who has been praying for hours for the son, "whom she still tried to visualize as in the arms of his Maker."

Immediately we pass to the final scene, which returns us to the massive, undifferentiated embodiment of the fundamental drama of the story, the scene of the Griffiths family lifting up their voices against the "tall walls of the commercial heart" of a great city—now San Francisco, and now with another child, the young grandson, among them. The fact of the repetition of the opening scene of the novel declares the issue—the issues—not to be brought to schematic focus, but to be regarded as continuously, and pervasively, present in life.

The complexity of Dreiser's attitude, something of the nature of the polarities of thought in his work, is indicated if we set against the novel the cinematic "treatment" written by the famous Sergei Eisenstein (now in the Eisenstein Collection in the Museum of Modern Art in New York City). Dreiser's presentation of Clyde as "innocent" was not satisfactory to a good Communist. In his book *Film Form* (Harcourt Brace, 1949), looking back on his work, Eisenstein writes:

> Dreiser's novel is as broad and shoreless as the Hudson; it is as immense as life itself, and allows almost any point of view on itself. Like every "neutral" fact of nature itself, his novel is ninety-nine percent statement of facts and one percent attitude toward them. This epic of cosmic veracity and objectivity had to be assembled in a tragedy—and this was unthinkable without a world-attitude of direction and point.

More specifically, Eisenstein objected to the fact that Dreiser had handled the episode of the murder as "an undifferentiated tangle," and had regarded it "so impartially that the further development of events is left formally, not to the logical course of the story, but to the "processes of law." So, to demonstrate the "monstrous challenge" of an evil society, Eisenstein set out to "sharpen the *actual* and *formal* innocence of Clyde within the very act of perpetrating the crime." Eisenstein does this by giving Clyde the very change of heart invented by Jephson, but there is some difference between Eisenstein's actual treatment and his later description of what he had intended. In the treatment, even though Clyde has had the change of heart, the emotional struggle shows in his face, with the pain of realizing that in sparing Roberta he is renouncing Sondra. The expression on his face evokes sympathy from Roberta, and as she crawls toward him and reaches to take his hand, he, with "an involuntary movement of revulsion . . . pulls back his hand and jumps up quickly," in the process "quite accidently [*sic*]" striking her. He does speak words of apology, and "makes a natural movement toward her," but she misinterprets this and, flinching from him, falls into the water, overturning the boat. In the water, Clyde does "make a movement to help Roberta," but she, now seeing the "terrible fright" on his face, "gives a piercing cry and, splashing frantically, disappears under the water." Eisenstein makes Clyde start to dive to save Roberta, but then Clyde "stops, and hesitates." This failure to act further is not interpreted by Eisenstein, but on the shore, Eisenstein creates a scene not given by Dreiser: Clyde lying with one foot still in the water, shivering and making a "familiar gesture, that gesture that he makes when frightened or suffering." Only now does he hear the voice of Eisenstein's interior dialogue, telling him that he has what he had sought, and only then does the thought of Sondra come—not, as in Dreiser, to prevent his helping Roberta in the water. Presumably, in the light of the emphasis on Clyde's fright even as he approaches Roberta, and of the gesture as he lies on the shore, we may take his failure to dive as the result of cowardice; the Efrit has not yet spoken.

If we consult Eisenstein's later discussion of his intentions, we find this account of the blow:

> . . . when he [Clyde] leans toward her [Roberta], already defeated inwardly and ready "to take everything back," she recoils from him in horror. The boat, off balance, rocks. When, in trying to support her, he accidentally knocks his camera against her face, she finally loses her head and in her terror, falls and the boat overturns.
>
> For greater emphasis we show her rising to the surface again. We even show Clyde trying to swim to her. But the

machinery of crime has been set in motion and continues to its end, even against Clyde's will. Roberta cries out weakly, tries to retreat from him in her horror, and, not being able to swim, drowns.

So much for Eisenstein's fairly thorough job of disinfecting Dreiser's ambiguities in the actual murder. But he does an even better job on the scene in the Governor's office, focusing, with sure dramatic and ideological instinct, on the mother, rather than on McMillan, as the betrayer of Clyde. It is she who, in purblind fanaticism, had fixed her "aim toward heaven rather than training her son for work." When Clyde confesses to her that, though he did not kill Roberta, he planned to do so, she, with the thought that sin in the heart is equivalent to sin in the act, is appalled. When, in the crucial scene, the Governor asks the same question that Dreiser's Governor directs to McMillan, she cannot speak. The mother's silence, as Eisenstein later summed up his intentions, discredits both the "dogma" that she embraces and her own "dogmatism," and the more moving her grief, the more that pathos impugns her ideology and that of society.

Even before Eisenstein had written his cinematic treatment, Dreiser had replied to political questions from another Communist, by giving the statement, already quoted, that life is "an organized process about which we can do nothing in the final analysis" and he had added that "dealing with man is a practical thing—not a theoretical one," and that "nothing can alter his emotions, his primitive and animal reactions to life." In the face of this statement, it may seem strange that Dreiser was, according to Eisenstein, "the first to salute all that had been brought to his work." But, on reflection, it is not strange at all—merely part and parcel of the tissue of polarities and paradoxes by which Dreiser lived and dealt with life.

Eisenstein's version was never produced—for good and sufficient reason. A treatment by Samuel Hoffenstein, though he apparently borrowed some of Eisenstein's devices for disinfecting Clyde in the murder scene, winds up with a mixed dose of bathos, dishonesty, and total confusion, with the mother and son embracing through the bars. The ghastly mess, directed by Josef von Sternberg, bears no slightest resemblance to the novel.

page 138

There is a remarkable resemblance between the doctrine of illusion in Dreiser and that in Conrad, for whom the illusion—the "Idea"—redeems all. Conrad's view is, of course, summed up in this famous passage from *Lord Jim*:

> A man that is born falls into a dream like a man who falls into the sea. If he tries to climb out into the air as inexperienced people endeavor to do, he drowns—*nicht wahr?* . . . No! I tell you! The way is to the destructive element submit yourself, and with the exertions of your hands and feet in the water make the deep, deep sea keep you up.

To paraphrase the passage: All men, by the mere fact of their being men and not animals, are dropped at birth into the "destructive element" strange to them—that is, into the necessarily human world of illusion, of dream, of "idea." Those men who deny their human fate, and try to interpret life "realistically" —that is, who try to return to the dry land of mere "nature," where animals live—drown in the "destructive element"; even if Gentleman Brown in *Lord Jim* tries to repudiate his humanity, his most vicious acts of destructive violence, such as the massacre of the Malays under Dain Waris, remain paradoxical affirmations of his human need for the "Idea," as is underscored by Conrad's remark that "even in this awful outbreak [of the massacre] there is a superiority as of a man who carries right—the abstract thing—within the envelope of his common desires."

Another strange association of Conrad and Dreiser appears through F. Scott Fitzgerald, who, as early as 1920, wrote defensively to the then President of Princeton that his philosophy was that of Conrad and Dreiser. It is easy to see how Fitzgerald was to go to school to Conrad, the master technician who made *The Great Gatsby* possible, but Dreiser is more difficult to explain. It may be argued that Dreiser the "realist" had given courage to the young Princetonian, even if the author of *This Side of Paradise* was about as far removed as possible from the author of *Sister Carrie*; or that, even though *An American Tragedy* did not appear until after *The Great Gatsby* was substantially written, Dreiser's earlier portraits of the young outsider touched a responsive chord in the heart of the young man from a side street in Saint Paul. But long before this Dreiser had already published *Sister Carrie* and the first two members of the Trilogy, and in those books the doctrine of illusion was fully illustrated and analyzed. Conrad, in addition to the fundamental lesson in the psychology of fictional form, could, of course, give Fitzgerald the general notion of the doctrine of illusion, but Dreiser had anchored that notion in

America, in the Middle West, and could anatomize it in detail. Behind Jim Gatz of North Dakota and the young Fitzgerald from Minnesota, stood Theodore Dreiser of Terre Haute, Indiana, another "Prince of Dreams."

page 139

The original manuscript of the novel—as with most of Dreiser's books—was much too long for publication, some million words. He turned the manuscript over, again as usual, to friends for editing, to Sally Russell and Louise Dudley, two of the several ladies who had a hand in the preparation of the novel. They cut it down to about half of the original bulk, and the publishers did further cutting. This process of composition makes criticism of Dreiser peculiarly difficult; for scale, pace, and proportion are, of course, significant factors in a work, and here is where the reader never knows the exact degree of Dreiser's responsibility for an effect. But clearly matters of basic structure, of character and psychology, and of thematic organization and interpretation are the work of Dreiser; and in one sense, he can be considered responsible for the finished product as a whole, for, after all, it was up to him to accept or reject cuts. He did, as a matter of fact, reject a substantial amount of cutting proposed by the publishers of *An American Tragedy*.

BIOGRAPHICAL SUMMARY

1871   Born, August 27, in Terre Haute, Indiana, son of John Paul Dreiser and Sarah Schänäb.

1879   Family broken up, never to be permanently reassembled; Dreiser and several children with mother in various localities—Vincennes, Sullivan, and Evansville.

1887–89 Dreiser in Chicago alone; menial labor in restaurant and hardware firm; found by Mildred Fielding, his old teacher.

1889–90 Indiana University, at Bloomington.

1890   Mother dies, November 14.

1892   Begins work as reporter on Chicago *Globe;* then St. Louis *Globe-Democrat* and *Republic.*

1893   Meets Sara White ("Jug").

1894   Newspaper work in Toledo, Cleveland, Pittsburgh.

1895   New York, with brother Paul Dresser; editor of *Ev'ry Month.*

1898   Marriage to Jug.

1899   Begins work on *Sister Carrie,* in Maumee, Ohio, while visiting Arthur Henry.

1900   Publication of *Sister Carrie,* by Doubleday, Page, and Company; failure.

1901–03 Increasing depression; first separation from Jug; nervous collapse; saved by Paul, who accidentally finds him and puts him on Muldoon's health farm.

1904–06 Resumes editorial career; Street and Smith magazines, *Smith's Magazine, Broadway Magazine.*

1906   Death of Paul.

1907   *Sister Carrie* republished, by B. W. Dodge and Company; beginning of literary success; becomes editor of Butterick publications—*Delineator, New Idea Woman's Magazine,* and *Designer.*

1909   *Jennie Gerhardt* begun.

1910   Fired, October 15, from Butterick editorship, on account of pursuit of Thelma Cudlipp, young daughter of a woman employee; full time on *Jennie Gerhardt.*

1911   *Jennie Gerhardt* published to respectful press; trip to Europe to gather material for Trilogy based on Charles Tyson Yerkes.

1912	*The Financier* published with moderate success; *Sister Carrie* again published, by Harper and Brothers; period in Chicago to do further research on Yerkes; acquaintance with literary and artistic group, including Edgar Lee Masters, Floyd Dell, Margaret Anderson, and actress Kirah Markham, who was to become a mistress.
1913	*A Traveler at Forty.*
1914	*The Titan,* published less successfully than *The Financier.*
1915	Automobile tour of Indiana, background for autobiographies; publication of *The "Genius."*
1916	*The "Genius"* banned for obscenity, and withdrawn; publicity and role of literary hero; *A Hoosier Holiday.*
1918	Dreiser's new publisher, Boni and Liveright, brings out *Free, and Other Stories, The Hand of the Potter* (play), and *Twelve Men* (sketches).
1919	Beginning liaison with Helen Patges Richardson; departure for Hollywood with Helen, beginning period there till late 1922; tentatively begins *An American Tragedy.*
1920	*Hey, Rub-A-Dub-Dub* (philosophical essays).
1922	*A Book About Myself* (autobiography) published, with miserable sale.
1923	Serious work on *An American Tragedy; The Color of a Great City* (sketches) published.
1925	*An American Tragedy* appears, with prodigious success; life of luxury.
1927	Visit to Russia; publication of *Chains* (stories).
1928	*Moods, Cadenced and Declaimed* (poems) and *Dreiser Looks at Russia.*
1929	*A Gallery of Women.*
1931	*Dawn* published, many years after composition; and *A Book about Myself* republished with new title *Newspaper Days; Tragic America.*
1932–34	Contributing editor of the *American Spectator,* edited by George Jean Nathan and Ernest Boyd.
1941	*America Is Worth Saving.*
1942	Death of Jug.
1944	Award of Merit by American Academy of Arts and Letters; marriage to Helen.
1945	Application for membership in Communist Party granted; death, in Hollywood, December 28; buried in Forest Lawn Cemetery.
1946	*The Bulwark.*
1947	*The Stoic,* last of the Trilogy.

BIBLIOGRAPHICAL NOTE

Among the early books on Dreiser several are still extremely useful: *Forgotten Frontiers: Dreiser and the Land of the Free*, by Dorothy Dudley (1932); *My Life with Dreiser*, by Helen Dreiser (1951); *Theodore Dreiser: Apostle of Nature*, by Robert H. Elias (1949), who worked closely with Dreiser in its preparation; and *Theodore Dreiser*, by F. O. Matthiessen (1951), a critical rather than a biographical work. *The Stature of Theodore Dreiser*, edited by Alfred Kazin and Charles Shapiro (1955), republishes probably all the important critical essays and comments of the early period. The last decade has seen a series of serious studies of Dreiser, including *Theodore Dreiser: Our Bitter Patriot*, by Charles Shapiro (1962), *Theodore Dreiser*, by Philip L. Gerber (1964), *Theodore Dreiser: An Introduction and Interpretation*, by John J. McAleer (1968), and *Theodore Dreiser: His World and His Novels*, by Richard Lehan (1969). Two recent books that deserve special comment are *Dreiser*, by W. A. Swanberg (1965), a massively documented biographical narrative, and *The Two Dreisers: The Man and the Novelist as Revealed in His Two Most Important Works*, by Ellen Moers (1969).

ABOUT THE AUTHOR

Robert Penn Warren was born in Guthrie, Kentucky, in 1905. After graduating *summa cum laude* from Vanderbilt University (1925), he received a master's degree from the University of California (1927), did graduate work at Yale University (1927–28) and then at Oxford as a Rhodes Scholar (B. Litt., 1930).

A list of Mr. Warren's books appears in the front of this volume. The variety of forms is extraordinary, including eight novels, nine volumes of poetry, short stories, a play, critical essays, a biography, a historical essay, and two studies of race relations in America. This body of work has been published in a period of thirty-nine years—a period during which Mr. Warren also had an active career as a professor of English. He is now a member of the faculty of Yale University.

All the King's Men (1946) was awarded the Pulitzer Prize for fiction. *Promises* (1957) won the Pulitzer Prize for poetry, the Edna St. Vincent Millay Prize of the Poetry Society of America, and the National Book Award. In 1944 Mr. Warren occupied the Chair of Poetry of the Library of Congress. In 1959 he was elected to the American Academy of Arts and Letters. In 1967 he received the Bollingen Prize in Poetry for *Selected Poems: New and Old, 1923–1966*, and in 1970 the National Medal for Literature.

Mr. Warren lives in Connecticut with his wife, Eleanor Clark (author of *Rome and a Villa, The Oysters of Locmariaquer*, and *Baldur's Gate*), and their two children, Rosanna and Gabriel.